RICHARD]
BRED TO B]

COVER PICTURES:

Front Cover: Richard Dunwoody holds the British National Hunt Jockeys' Championship trophy after winning the title for the first time at the end of the 1992-'93 season (Picture: Colin Turner).

Back Cover: Richard Dunwoody with Martin Pipe at the outset of the 1993-'94 National Hunt Season. Dunwoody had succeeded Peter Scudamore as No. 1 jockey at the Pipe stable after Scu announced his retirement from the saddle in April, 1993 (Picture: Colin Turner).

By the same Author:

Winner Alright – Bred In Northern Ireland (1985)

RICHARD DUNWOODY
BRED TO BE CHAMPION

By
JIMMY WALKER

SPORTING BOOKS PUBLISHERS
DUBLIN
1993

RICHARD DUNWOODY
BRED TO BE CHAMPION

Copyright: JIMMY WALKER, 1993

Published by: Sporting Books Publishers, Dublin.

Print origination and typesetting by:
The City Office, Dublin 2.

Printed by: The Leinster Leader, Naas.

CONTENTS

AUTHOR'S NOTE

by

JIMMY WALKER

Northern Ireland from an extremely small population has produced quite a number of outstanding sporting personalities, some of whom have risen to the very pinnacle in their various fields, forging reputations that have circled the globe and stood the test of time.

Richard Dunwoody, John Reid and Ray Cochrane, to name but three, have shown that when it comes to the world of racing, then the Province has the ability to produce something really special and this, of course, is true of Ireland as a whole.

I had at first decided to write a book encompassing the lives and times of Dunwoody, Reid and Cochrane. But as the 1992-'93 National Hunt season progressed it became obvious that Dunwoody was going to win the British jockeys' championship and the way was finally cleared for him to assume the crown when Peter Scudamore announced to a stunned racing world in April '93 that he was retiring.

So I concentrated on Dunwoody and hopefully the others will eventually get their turn.

In writing the "Richard Dunwoody Story" I have first of all to thank Richard himself for his assessments of the outstanding horses he has ridden in recent years and also his father George – in his time one of Northern Ireland's most likeable and successful amateur riders and trainers – for the ready co-operation he afforded me in this project.

In addition, my good friend Jimmy Burgess, who was almost a part of the Dunwoody family, and who was extremely helpful, and, in fact, gave me the start on the story which I needed.

Other well-known Northern Ireland racing personalities – Dessie Osborne, Will Martin and Billy Patton – supplied invaluable recollections and Lambourn trainer, Terry Casey very kindly gave me a large portion of his time and put some of the early pieces into place.

Billy Patton also supplied pictures of George Dunwoody at point-to-points in the Sixties while Richard's school teacher, Kay McIlveen was helpful in letting me have a personal autographed picture of Richard Dunwoody after he had won the 1986 Grand National on West Tip.

Terry Hill and his wife Betty were also extremely kind in lending me snapshots from family albums.

In addition, many trainers, jockeys and racing personalities – too numerous to thank individually, but quoted in the book – provided their assessments and personal recollections of Dunwoody the jockey and this has helped me to incorporate stimulating material for debate in a book which I hope will be of more than passing interest to the racing fraternity.

However, pride of place as far as my thanks is concerned must go to my good friend, Raymond Smith, Editor of the *Irish Racing Annual,* who took on the project and edited it into shape. He was enthusiastic from the outset about the concept of a biography of Richard Dunwoody when I broached the subject to him and encouraged me in every way possible while bringing his own knowledge and experience of the book trade into play to ensure that the pre-Christmas deadline for publication would be met.

Without Raymond's guidance and the work of *Belfast Telegraph* secretary, Angela Klein, who typed the manuscript, this book would still be lying dormant in the back of my mind. I should also like to pay a special tribute to *Belfast Telegraph* librarian, Walter Macauley for his unfailing courtesy and also to Eugene Webber, News Librarian of the Press Association Library, Fleet Street for his valued assistance.

The fact that the book has come to life is due to these people and also to the encouragement and support of my wife Iris, whose optimism at just the right moments helped smooth many a rough path.

I would like to pay special tribute to Maurice Moore of Independent Newspapers who designed the cover.

Finally, I should like to thank Julian Wilson of the BBC for supplying the Foreword. I have known Julian for many years and I must say that his knowledge of the racing game is second to none.

It is timely, I feel, that Richard Dunwoody's attainment of his first jockeys' championship to supplement his outstanding riding successes, in particular his victories in the Grand National, Gold Cup and Champion Hurdle should be marked by a biography to chronicle these achievements for lovers of National Hunt Racing.

JIMMY WALKER

FOREWORD

by

Julian Wilson
of the BBC

The rise of Richard Dunwoody has been as enjoyable to spectate as it was easy to predict. The guidance and selflessness of Richard's parents George and Gillian have fashioned a supreme sportsman, and a thoroughly likeable individual.

It was Richard's grey 12.2.hh. pony Tony, a Connemara/Welsh cross-bred that guided the future Champion through his formative riding years. Loaned from the Dunwoody's next-door neighbours, the Mitchells, in Co. Down, he accompanied the family to Gloucestershire in the late '60s and gave Richard many exciting days with the Beaufort Hunt. He served Richard faithfully for eight years, until the age of 12.

It was racing's gain when Richard, having secured a scholarship to Rencome College, decided to deviate from his original intention to pursue veterinary science and espouse race riding.

His period riding out for trainer Ben Hanbury when the family moved to Newmarket in 1977, set the seal on his ambition.

Richard was always an intense young man, a characteristic that created a brief crisis during his schooling – and his single-minded determination inspired the nick-name "Mr. Angry" in his early weighing-room days.

He viewed the old-fashioned jockey's lifestyle of all-night parties and a midday "Sharpener" as unprofessional and dangerous. "A clear eye sees a true stride", was his firm philosophy. He has reaped the fruits of his self-denial.

Richard's professional coming-of-age came with his link-up with the equally single-minded disciplinarian David Nicholson in 1986. Big race triumphs with Charter Party, Another Coral and Very Promising established both men at the pinnacle.

He is blessed with a charming and lively wife in Carol. Carol was reared in the delightful Berkshire village of Baulking Green. The horse of that name, owned by local farmer Jim Reade, spent the summer months in my home village of Little Coxwell, while his owner and the writer fielded slip and gully respectively for Faringdon Cricket Club!

Richard remains the professional's professional; the supreme stylist; and a young man of integrity and delightful manners. N.H. racing is the richer for his presence at the top.

CHAPTER 1

THE SUPREME STYLIST

"*A*nd *it's Richard Dunwoody the youngest jockey in the race, on West Tip, winning the 1986 Grand National . . . .*"
The unmistakable tones of Peter O'Sullevan, the 'Voice of the BBC', calling the finishing stages of the world's most famous steeplechase did more than just make sure the name of the 22-year-old winning jockey would be known within minutes in every home in the land. O'Sullevan also provided the first nationwide recognition that here was a startlingly new talent and that Northern Ireland, in addition to spawning legendary footballers, hard-as-nails boxers, high-speed motor cycle road racers and controversial snooker players, could also turn out heroes in the racing game.

But more than that . . . O'Sullevan was announcing the era of a new icon – Richard Dunwoody, the supreme stylist , who would go on seven years later to reach the peak of his profession in 1993 when he realised his great ambition by becoming National Hunt Champion jockey in Britain and one week later was awarded the MBE in the Queen's Birthday Honours.

The sudden retirement before the end of the 1992-'93 National Hunt season of eight-times champion jockey, Peter Scudamore ensured that

Dunwoody would become jump racing's 'King', a position he intends to hold for a long time to come.

Square jawed, fair haired and equipped with an unblinking gaze, Dunwoody has the look of a finely honed athlete. On meeting him you might take him for a professional tennis player or even a tough tackling member of the back four in a rugby squad. In fact, the man simply exudes fitness.

His polite, always attentive and articulate manner has made him an interviewer's dream. It is no coincidence that on the major occasions he is always sought out by the seemingly endless battery of radio and television journalists.

After any big race it's always a case of "Is Richard in there?" And invariably the attendant at the weighroom door has to deliver yet another message to Dunwoody who, with a quick comb of the hair and a swift look in the mirror, emerges cool, calm and almost casual for a routine which he must by now know by heart.

I'm always amazed that he never shows the slightest sign of impatience with anyone, even when he has every good reason to duck out of sight and collect his thoughts. He is never rude. He appears to have time for everyone and, to be honest, I couldn't picture him ever being caught off guard.

Of course, being a top athlete with impeccable manners doesn't guarantee sporting success. You need a lot more than that. Talent for one thing and that indefinable will to win which so many sportsmen seem to lack when it comes to the crunch.

Not so Dunwoody. When you see him looming up about to launch his assault in the closing stages of a race, you are privileged to watch a real professional at work.

I remember talking to Ulsterman Paddy Graffin, one of Ireland's leading amateur riders, when he was riding at the 1990 Cheltenham Festival meeting. During what could be termed a "rest period", he took a stroll to the last fence to view the finish of the Queen Mother Champion Chase.

Dunwoody was on Waterloo Boy and Hywel Davies on Barnbrook Again. This race has gone into history. David Nicholson, trainer of Waterloo Boy who was beaten, said: "You won't see a better race than that and Richard has rarely ridden a finer one."

As for Graffin, he told me: "Just to stand at that fence and watch Dunwoody and Davies throwing everything into all or nothing efforts made me feel privileged to be in the same sport. I've never felt excitement like it. Those two are MEN."

Unfortunately, the stewards didn't see it the same way and banned both for excessive use of the whip. But more about this later, for the whip guidelines have been a constant bone of contention, not only for Dunwoody but other top steeplechase jockeys. Dunwoody, although beaten that day, showed once again that he gives his all in a finish, so what more could you ask for – and his courage is unquestioned also, as he proved when winning the Aintree Grand National on West Tip. He has no superior among modern day jockeys when it comes to the test of horsemanship in the world's most famous steeplechase.

I recall at Aintree some years back meeting legendary professional gambler, the late Alec Bird who had won and lost fortunes on this most fascinating of races. I spoke to him in that little alley between the weighroom and the unsaddling enclosure where many go to see others to be seen.

Anyway, after Mike Torpey, a good friend of mine from the *Liverpool Echo,* had introduced us, I rather nervously asked Alec what he fancied for the National two days later.

"I don't follow the form for this race nowadays," he told me. "I can only give you this advice. Back Dunwoody, for he is the best National jockey I have seen and I can go back a few years."

Dunwoody had already won on West Tip a year earlier but within forty-eight hours of Alec Bird's prediction he had given yet another superb exhibition of horsemanship and jockeyship when he took West Tip into fourth place behind Maori Venture.

There are some cynics who would pose the question: "If Dunwoody is so good why did he take so long to be Champion jockey?"

Well, look at it this way. Gordon Richards won over 4,000 races on the Flat and was champion jockey 26 times. Lester Piggott came nowhere near that record but in big races – Epsom Derby most of all – while Gordon struggled, Lester reigned supreme.

To my mind Dunwoody is Piggott to Scudamore's Richards. Scudamore who retired four days after the infamous 1993 void Grand National, landed only one of the Big Three jump races – the Gold Cup, Champion Hurdle and the National. Dunwoody by then had not only grabbed them all, he was already looking for repeats.

Scudamore – an outstanding National Hunt jockey in his own right and a born gentleman – first became aware of the young Dunwoody when

4

Richard rode what is now an almost legendary four-timer at Hereford in March 1984.

"I wasn't at the meeting for I was riding at the Grand National fixture," he told me, "but I realised that here we had a new talent which could shake quite a few of us, although at that time of course I had no idea that he would go so far."

Scudamore and Dunwoody eventually became the top two contestants for the British Jockeys Championship, slogging it out every year with Scu always winning until he decided in April, 1993 – when he was 17 behind Dunwoody in the title race – that enough was enough and to the consternation of almost every punter in the country he packed it in.

"Of course I'll miss the camaraderie of the jockey's room and particularly Richard, for we travelled all over the world together and were always good friends," he said. "America, New Zealand, Australia – we had great memories.

"I reckon that more than anything else I respected him for his style of riding. He is a dedicated professional who loves the sport and more important its public image. This can be gauged through his admirably quick statement after the fracas in the Plaza Hotel in London following the jockeys awards."

Scudamore was referring to an incident in March 1993 when Dunwoody and another jockey, Roger Marley, were arrested at 5.45 a.m. for disorderly behaviour after attending the Jockeys Association awards dinner, where Dunwoody had been voted No. 1. They were freed with a caution 3½ hours later.

After the incident in the hotel, Dunwoody

issued a statement to the Press Association stating he regretted the whole matter "and the adverse publicity it might have brought to the ceremony and my profession."

"I was upset at Roger's arrest and this unfortunately led to my own," he added.

According to Scudamore the whole affair was blown up out of all proportion "but Richard was right to try to maintain the dignity of a profession of which he is fiercely proud," he said.

"There is no doubt that he is highly respected by other jockeys in the weighroom and I feel it is also fair to say that he is also very well liked. Just one of the boys, you might say.

"His total dedication has made him what might appear to be a very private person and one who is hard to get to know but this was never the case with me personally and I have always found him a close friend, although there was a lot of cut and thrust, as both of us liked to win.

"At the same time though we tried to help each other. And I remember one occasion at Ludlow when we were both going for the Jockeys Championship and Richard came out to the start without his goggles. I had decided to go off in front so I lent him mine. Unfortunately, I missed the break and ended up at the rear of the field with my eyes filled with mud!"

Scudamore added that he would always remember the driving Dunwoody style which brought him victory on so many occasions and he was particularly pleased to recall the day when riding Pearlyman he beat Dunwoody on Waterloo Boy in the Two Miles Champion Chase at Cheltenham. "I still think that was one of my best rides as there was nothing in it at the finish," he told me.

"On another occasion, however, Richard beat me on Remittance Man over hurdles at Cheltenham when I felt I might have won on Regal Ambition. He was always a hard man to get the better of in a finish.

"I'm delighted that of all jockeys he is the one who has taken over as champion. You know, he might have had the title earlier in his career. You may remember I was out for 10 weeks with a broken leg a few years ago and I thought I had no chance of catching Richard. Well, I did and I know Richard was bitterly disappointed at losing out on that occasion, although he is much too dignified a man to ever show his feelings.

"Now that he is champion I can see him being there for a long time."

CHAPTER 2

BORN INTO RACING

Richard Dunwoody was born into racing and bred to be a champion one day. His father George, from Monaghan, was one of Northern Ireland's best known and most successful amateur riders who also made a living as a trainer, while Richard's mother, Gillian was the daughter of Epsom trainer Dick Thrale.

Even the house in Co. Down where the young Dunwoody was brought up dripped with racing tradition. It was owned by Frank Shane who had bred the 1957 Epsom Derby runner-up Paddy's Point, the 100/1 chance ridden by Willie Robinson, who followed home Lester Piggott on the favourite Crepello. Paddy's Point, in fact, was named after a headland near the Dunwoody home at Ringneill, Comber.

Owner and breeder Jimmy Burgess, a lifelong friend of the family who still flies to England for many of Dunwoody's races, remembers the early days well.

"I had known George through following the point to points and I met Gillian when she came over from England to hunt with Major Michael O'Reilly at Dromara in County Down," he said. "I was a close friend of amateur rider Will Martin, cousin of Raymond Martin who later won fame when riding Call Collect at Aintree and Cheltenham. Will rode in the point to points with Major O'Reilly and George and Gillian were very much a part of the racing and hunting scene there in those days."

After their marriage George and Gillian moved to Comber where they looked after the mares owned by Frank Shane. It was while they were at Paddy's Point that young Dunwoody was born, although he actually first saw the light of day in a Belfast nursing home.

Before moving to the Shane house, George had trained for a while at Ballyclare in County Antrim from the home later owned by veterinary surgeon and trainer Davy Clyde (incidentally, Davy's stallion, Silver Cloud sired the 1982 Cheltenham Gold Cup winner Silver Buck who was bred nearby).

George Dunwoody, Willie Rooney – holder of the record number of point to point winners at 401 – Frankie Fitzsimmons, Will Martin, John Agnew, now a National Hunt steward, Maurice and Roddy Bamber and Willie and Sammy Patton . . . these were the big names between the flags in those days and George Dunwoody was among the best of them, carving out a fine reputation as an amateur rider.

Jimmy Burgess was one of the owners George rode for and it meant he was the regular jockey on a highly successful horse named Zell. But there was one occasion when George wasn't exactly flavour of the month with Jimmy. That was when Zell was beaten at Leopardstown.

George had won a bumper on Zell at Mullingar and was expected to follow up at the Dublin track but Waring Willis, another fine amateur of the old school and later a trainer, stole a march on him and at one stage had poached a lead of 20 lengths.

George had reduced this to a couple of lengths at the finish, but Jimmy was less than pleased.

Shortly afterwards Gillian rang Jimmy up and asked him innocently: "What happened to George?"

The answer wasn't long in coming. "What happened?" the disgruntled Burgess bellowed. "Tell him if he wants to fall asleep to try someone else's horse!"

George trained Zell and another good horse named Flashing, owned by Belfast accountant Roley Savage, at a time when he had moved to show jumper Billy McCully's place at Carrowdore in County Down and had begun to train again following Frank Shane's death.

Richard had by now started riding out with his father when he was only five years old on a pony named Tony. As it turned out, this pony helped him to develop the style which he has now made his own.

Apart from Zell and Flashing, among the many other winners turned out by George Dunwoody at Carrowdore was Rotomar Girl, owned by motor trader David Prentice, whose win at Gowran Park is one of Richard's earliest memories of the racing game.

"I was only seven at the time but I wanted that mare to win so badly so that I could lead her in," he told me.

Burgess, too, has had his moments as a breeder and 15 years on he must have had mixed feelings as he watched Richard parade on West Tip before the start of the 1986 National. For Jimmy had bred another of the runners, Door Latch, also at Comber, and Door Latch who had won two SGB Chases at Ascot was one of the fancied runners.

However, Jimmy's conflict of interests soon ended when Door Latch fell at the first and no one cheered louder when Richard Dunwoody brought West Tip home a winner.

A man also closely involved in the formative years of Richard Dunwoody was Terry Casey, now a Lambourn-based jump trainer. A Donegal man, Terry used to ride for Richard's father and in one highly memorable season, 1967-68, he rode all George's jumping winners, including the remarkable Aldave owned by David Prentice and named after David and his brother Albert. This is the horse who launched the Prentice career in racing and was bought in a field at Ballyhackamore, Belfast, from Billy McDonald, who went on to win fame as the member of the Robert Sangster team who bought the dual Arc winner Alleged for Sangster and Vincent O'Brien.

McDonald registered the Prentice colours with the Irish Turf Club and Casey was successful on this hurdler four times – at Navan, Down Royal, Dundalk and Baldoyle.

Terry first met George at Navan races one Saturday afternoon and it all came about because of an advertisement for stable staff in the *Irish Field*.

He had finished his apprenticeship with Aubrey Brabazon on the Curragh and was looking for work. He spotted George Dunwoody's advertisement and, as he wanted to join a small jumping stable, he reckoned this was for him. He was also attracted by the fact that the stable was in

12

Northern Ireland, for which he had a particular liking.

When Dunwoody met Casey at Navan he informed him that the post he had been after had been filled, but that Billy McCully, George's landlord at Kilbright House, was looking for someone to ride out his showjumpers and if a deal could be arrived at Casey would also be able to ride out for George. Casey takes up the story:

"Shortly afterwards I travelled to Belfast on the train from Dublin and George met me at the old Great Northern Railway Station in Great Victoria Street before taking me on to McCully's place at Movilla, Newtownards. It was there that I lived for over a year and spent some of the happiest days of my racing career, riding out along the beaches of Strangford Lough on the Ards Peninsula. Beautiful countryside and highly hospitable people."

The young Dunwoody, who had been born on January 18, 1964, was only a fledgling in those days, but when Terry left the Dunwoodys and went to Monaghan to join Bobby Patton who trained there, he still kept in touch with George and Gillian and rode out for them twice a week despite the long drive from the Border country.

"At that time, too, I was able to race ride, and one of the most successful horses was Zell on whom I won three hurdle races," Terry added.

Zell also won two bumpers, one of them with George Dunwoody up at Mullingar as mentioned earlier and the other with that fine horseman, now a successful trainer, Francis Flood in the saddle at Balduyle.

Terry remembers young Richard riding out also on his pony which he schooled over the odd hedge or two in addition to using the jumping ring which George had built.

"Richard did have remarkable ability even at that early age," Terry said. "In fact, he used to fly round the jumping course and it was quite obvious he was going to be a race rider if he retained his enthusiasm."

Terry also recalled that on one occasion when George and Gillian were on holiday Terry was left to keep an eye on the house. The young Dunwoody was being looked after by a friend of the family. However, Terry was still able to ride out with him and no doubt some of his skills rubbed off, although this most modest of men would never say so.

Will Martin remembers that holiday as well. "I used to come down from Ballynahinch to help out most mornings and young Richard was always about the place," he said. "But the time I remember most was when I would take horses down to the beach at Newtownards and meet George coming from Carrowdore. Both of us would ride out our strings at the same time and Richard would of course come along on his pony.

"When we had pulled up we would stop and look round for Richard who, of course, couldn't keep up with us. However, I can tell you that he had grim determination, crouched down behind the pony's head like Martin Molony in his prime.

"I thought to myself there and then: 'If he has the brain, he most certainly has the style.' Well, he has since proved beyond any shadow of doubt that he has the brain as well."

Brains and ability. These were the qualities Dessie Osborne, for many years Secretary and Joint

Master of North Down Harriers, noted about the young Dunwoody in the late sixties and early seventies.

"Of course, he was only a kid and no one would have dreamed about the heights he was going to achieve as a jockey," he said. "I used to ride as an amateur for George with a certain amount of success so I got to know the Dunwoodys very well. I'll always remember Richard's mother who appeared to be the driving force in the family. And perhaps this is where Richard gets his determination. You know Gillian was working about the horses and still riding out even when heavily pregnant with Richard.

"I recall one day going to the races with George and Gillian, with George driving and Gillian in the passenger seat while I was in the back with the horses and trailer. I felt at the time that we might have to stop somewhere along the road and deliver the baby there and then. That would have been some story . . . Richard Dunwoody born on the way to Baldoyle races!

"I became acquainted with George when he had broken his leg while down at Carrowdore and I used to ride amateur for him. I rode a few winners too but I'll always remember my biggest success was inadvertently due to George.

"He had a mare called Lesson Too, a useful one which I used to ride out on, and it was to race at Navan. I could do the weight of 11-1 and was naturally hoping for the ride.

"But George decided to put John Fowler up and the mare duly obliged. I was disappointed but I held no bitterness, for George and I have always been the best of friends.

"Anyway, Punchestown Festival was next on the horizon and George had a horse called Snow Lodge in the Ladies Cup over the Bank course. I fancied my chances on Snow Lodge on whom I had already won in a point to point, but Leslie Crawford, who trained near Belfast, also had a horse in the race called Straight Ahead and I rode for Leslie in those days too. To be honest, the fact that I had missed the mount on Lesson Too at Navan more or less made up my mind for me and I chose Crawford's horse and managed to win. It's funny the way things turn out in racing.

"Snow Lodge also provided me with a sharp memory of the young Dunwoody. At Lisnalinchy point to point I was down to ride two horses for George and Snow Lodge was one of them. After I had won on Snow Lodge and was about to dismount, Richard came over to inform me that I was now going to ride the good horse! Well, even in those early days I respected his judgement but unfortunately my second horse fell so I never knew how good it was.

"On the hunting field Richard always looked at home on his pony, although George, who brought him to our meetings, was at pains to make sure he got round safely, naturally enough. Well, he needn't have worried for on one occasion after we had jumped a hedge we looked round and there was no sign of Richard. So we went back thinking we would find him lying there but instead Richard had decided to pick his own spot to jump and was by now well up with the rest of the hunt. We knew then that he didn't need a nursemaid.

"It was no surprise to me when in later years he made such great strides as a jockey, although

16

Gillian wanted him to be a vet. I remember her saying to me on many occasions: 'I don't want him to have a career riding horses. My plan is to put him into veterinary college.'

"Well, circumstances dictated differently for shortly afterwards the family left Northern Ireland for good and I must say that I for one missed the company and the expertise of George, for he was one of our finest horsemen and even won a hurdle race at Down Royal on Flashing when he must have been in his fifties. A gifted rider whose skills have most certainly been passed on to some effect."

George Dunwoody was also a good man at organising a coup as Dessie Osborne was able to tell me.

"I never rode Zell in a race, but I used to take over on the gallops on the shores of Strangford Lough," he recalled.

On one occasion when George Dunwoody was getting Zell ready for that race at Baldoyle which he won with Francis Flood up, Dessie was down to gallop him and afterwards Jimmy Burgess came over and asked him how it had gone. Dessie didn't know that Jimmy was the owner or even part-owner as may have been the case, so he said nothing.

"I had raced against another horse with George up, in the gallop, but I was carrying a stone and a half more than George was and had finished close behind his mount so I knew pretty well what I had in hand," Dessie said. "I kept my mouth shut even when Burgess persisted in trying to get some information from me."

The following weekend they set out for Baldoyle

with Francis Flood booked. The money was down and Zell duly obliged. However, a surprised Osborne suddenly saw that Burgess was in the ring and obviously very much a part of the gamble. "I apologised to him but he told me he was delighted with the way in which I had handled his questions and gave me a present as my part of the deal," Dessie recalled. "George could certainly get one ready. That was for sure."

Francis Flood could verify that, and he told me about another day at the Fairyhouse Irish National meeting when a Burgess-owned horse was running.

The horse was Door Girl and was trained initially in the North with no significant success. Flood advised Jimmy to bring it South and he did so, to Noel Sleator's yard at Grangecon, Co. Wicklow.

Noel doesn't train now but he's a cousin of Paddy Sleator and the father of amateur rider John Sleator. Anyway, Noel got the horse ready, Flood rode it and George Dunwoody was also in on the gamble. The boys landed a brilliant "touch", backing it all the way from 14/1 to 2/1 favourite.

"Jimmy and George were always great friends of mine even though Jimmy's liking for a gamble sometimes put the pressure on!" said Flood. "I still see George a lot when I'm over at Cheltenham and I reminisce about old times. He's a real gentleman, I can tell you, a man with a very easy going temperament."

John Fowler, one of Ireland's top amateurs before turning trainer in the late Seventies, was another who was part of the Dunwoody set-up. "It was my father who began the link," said the man who trained Maid of Money to win the 1989 Irish Grand National. "he had a lot of horses in training and he used George Dunwoody from time to time."

One horse Fowler will always remember is Bald Face, for he was a polo pony in the summer and a point to pointer in the winter!

Brigadier Fowler, John's father, used to ride him in polo matches at the Phoenix Park and then when winter came along he was turned to the points where George Dunwoody came on the scene usually to good effect.

John Fowler never managed to win the Irish amateur championship, although he was second on a number of occasions. Ted Walsh and Dermot Weld seemed to dominate this, but Dunwoody gave him plenty of chances on his horses and John rode a lot of winners for him.

"Richard, of course, is something else," John enthused. "I regard him as the best horseman in the British Isles with the only possible contenders Charlie Swan and Mark Dwyer. If I were looking for a top pilot these are the ones I would call on in that order."

He didn't mention Adrian Maguire and this seemed to strike a chord when I asked him why not. "He's not a horseman in the real sense," he told me. "He certainly has ridden a lot of winners but he's not the sort of man I would call on. If you are looking for a man to get the best out of your horse then you have to send for Dunwoody."

Another top amateur rider with reason to remember Richard Dunwoody is Raymund Martin, who enjoyed an Indian summer in 1989 and 1990 through the exploits of the star hunter chaser, Call Collect.

Martin, who now trains at Ballynahinch, County Down, was still race riding at 49 years of age, although he wasn't so much in the thick of it as when he was a leading contender for the Ulster point to point jockeys championship in the Sixties and Seventies before he eventually clinched the title in 1982.

Martin's career in the saddle spanned two decades and that has given him the edge over most when it comes to describing at first hand the Northern Ireland National Hunt scene over the past 25 years. Because of his length of time in the saddle Martin could also claim an unusual distinction – he was the only race rider still operating in 1993 to have ridden against both George and Richard Dunwoody.

Raymund rode regularly against George in the late Sixties when he was training at Carrowdore and 20 years later rode against Richard in the 1990 National.

But one spring day in 1970 still sticks in Martin's mind – not so much for his encounters with George, memorable though they might have been, but for the fact that it was the first time he set eyes on the young Dunwoody. Of all places it was in the casualty tent at North Down Harriers point to point at Craigantlet on the outskirts of Belfast.

Martin was riding a horse called Vulgan's Image. They were beginning the final circuit of the race when a horse ridden by John Stirling jumped across him and Martin cannoned into another horse ridden by Bertie Poots. Both jockeys went down and were rushed to casualty. Martin had a punctured lung and two broken ribs and Bertie had a broken jaw.

As they went into the casualty tent there at the head of the queue was young Dunwoody. He must have been about six years old then and he had been taken there for treatment after having tripped on a guy rope at one of the marquees. He was next in line for attention but Martin was taken to the head of the queue, so of course Richard had to wait.

Twenty years later that incident came into Martin's mind again as he lined up against Richard in the 1990 National. Martin was riding Call Collect and Dunwoody was on Bigsun. "I have often wondered if he remembers that day but I have never been in his company often enough to bring the matter up," Raymund said.

That Grand National, by coincidence, saw the wheel turn the full circle, for Dunwoody finished sixth and Martin seventh only one and a half lengths behind. That day it was Dunwoody's turn at the head of the queue!

"I've always admired his style," Martin told me. "His father was a tough competitor, although hard and fair. He rode with the 'armchair' style as opposed to the streamline version of race riding we see from the young Dunwoody. They are worlds apart in this respect but there's no doubt where Richard gets his talent from. I can see him being a champion for a long time for he appears to have everything."

Terence McKeag, another member of the point to point set in County Down, would agree that Dunwoody is similar to his father in a lot of ways. "He has the same astute manner as George," he told me. "One summer during holidays from my

21

job with the shirt factory owned by former Northern Ireland Premier Brian Faulkner, I spent ten continuous days driving mares to and from the Shane Stud at Comber to Kildare and elsewhere. George was the Stud Manager then and you had to know your job when he was around. Richard strikes me as having the same business-like mind and perhaps that's one of the reasons for his success."

Kay McIlveen, a schoolmistress who lives close to the sleepy County Down village of Carrowdore, may not know much about the racing skills which Richard Dunwoody developed, but she could certainly vouch for his keen brain for she taught him for the first three years of his schooling career.

Kay, who now lives in retirement beside Dunover Primary School, which sadly is no longer used, told me: "I remember Richard coming to us when he was four years old. He had a marvellous personality even then and very soon he looked to me to have the potential for an academic career. The Principal of the school, May Lyttle, confirmed this one day when she told me that she felt Richard could make it to the top and, like myself, she was sad when he eventually left us.

"Of course, he always had a mad passion for horses. But we knew the family he had come from and expected this. We didn't discourage him. On the contrary, whenever a race meeting at Downpatrick – our nearest course – would come along or it was Grand National or Derby week we would encourage young Dunwoody in one of his special projects which always involved horse racing. We used to get into small discussion groups even though the youngsters were only around five and six years old. It was delightful to look back on."

Richard stayed at Dunover School for almost four years. He moved on to the upper school taught by May Lyttle before his parents decided it was time to leave for England. "I think he was sad to leave us," Kay told me. "You know he had a pet rabbit and he asked one of his close friends, John Kennedy, to look after it for him."

For the two teachers of this tiny school of only 54 pupils it was a double blow when the Dunwoodys left for Richard's sister Gail, who had just joined Dunover and was in the first form, had obviously to leave as well. So there's no knowing what careers the young Dunwoodys would have taken up if they had stayed in Northern Ireland.

But that's life . . . and the hinge of Fate. Still, Dunwoody is not one to forget his roots and he kept in touch with his old schoolmistress over the years as he grew up to become a jockey and eventually the champion over the jumps.

"I watched his career with interest," Kay told me, "but I never got the chance to see him in person again, although I came close to it on one occasion.

"Back in 1986 when he was over to ride at Down Royal he and his mother, who were visiting relatives, made an unexpected visit to see Miss Lyttle and myself but unfortunately we were both out at the time. Still, Richard wanted us to know he had been there so he posted through the door a note along with two pictures of him winning the Grand National that year.

"These will always be among my most treasured possessions."

Katy McIlveen may have missed out on the Dunwoody visit home, but John Kennedy didn't. The youngster who had been entrusted with Richard's pet rabbit was by now a strapping farmer in his early twenties when he bumped into Dunwoody and his mother shopping in Newtownards, County Down, just after Dunwoody had won the National.

"I couldn't believe it," he told me. "Richard had by now become something of a household name and I was delighted that he still recognised me. It brought back a lot of memories of old times together.

"You know, although we grew up during what has become known as the beginning of 'The Troubles', we were totally unaware of them, except through the television. In fact, had it not been for the 'box' we wouldn't have realised what was happening in Belfast and yet we were only 22 miles away.

"The school which Richard and I attended had only two classrooms but it was a quiet, old world country way of life which we enjoyed. Our school was so small, in fact, that we had no canteen and the meals had to be brought to us specially in a van!

"Richard was always keen on horses and animals generally and used to come round to my house to see our farm. I always remember him riding his pony but that rabbit was also something of a special pet. Snowy was its name and when Richard left us to go to England he entrusted Snowy into my care. For years afterwards when he would write to us he always asked how Snowy was progressing. I kept that rabbit nine years.

"Richard would have been too young for our soccer team which was late in forming simply because we didn't have enough pupils of the right age. We used to kick a ball about, of course, but our chief hobby would have been the nature walks when we wrote down the names of the various trees and collected chestnuts.

"I remember Richard was a modest, good-mannered friend who I suppose was somewhat reserved compared to some of the other pupils.

"He always appeared to be a thinker and I must say we all missed him when he left.

"Still, although I have no interest in racing, when Richard is riding in a race on television I make a point of watching. It gives me something of a kick to recall that someone from our tiny country school has become so famous."

CHAPTER 3

GROWING UP IN 'THE TROUBLES'

The idyllic world in which Richard Dunwoody grew up might as well have been on another planet for all the resemblance it bore to what was happening in large urban areas of Northern Ireland, particularly Belfast at the time.

For the early Seventies marked the height of the civil unrest in the Province, euphemistically called 'The Troubles'.

While Dunwoody's father and other members of the racing fraternity hunted, tended their horses and went about their business on the racecourses of Ireland, and Richard himself played about as any other child would, there was rioting, shooting and violence in Belfast, merging into bombings that seemed in time to become never-ending.

The polarisation of the two communities was emphasised sadly in the shells of burnt-out homes. That fine Northern Ireland poet, John Hewitt (died 1987) looking at the tragedy with the same eye that a Yeats or Kavanagh might have viewed it, penned at the height of the strife lines that would echo for all time the pain and the suffering of innocent victims of the violence who simply asked: When will we see some light at the end of the tunnel?

The night-sky red, crackle and roar of flame,
the barricades across the ruined street,
the thump of stones, the shots, the thudding feet;
as mob greets mob with claim and counterclaim,
each blames the other, none accepts the blame,
for fears entrenched will not permit retreat,
when fears and creed inhospitably meet,
and each child's fate foreshadowed in its name.

So fare our cities in this year of grace,
sick with old poisons seeped from history;
frustration on one side, the other fear
sodden with guilt. To their embattled place
the stubborn masters cling, while year by year
from this infection no man's blood runs free.

The civil unrest in the Province had begun in 1969 on a serious scale and for the next three years there were major shifts in population as residents of certain areas moved to centres where they felt safer.

It was an urban "sea change" which no one could remember having seen before and the natural consequences was that it added to the polarisation of two communities.

Yet despite 'The Troubles', sport in the Province continued incredibly almost uninterrupted and racing especially was carried on as though nothing was happening at all. In many ways it was a bizarre situation and in retrospect seems almost unreal as I reflect on it over twenty years later.

Northern Ireland has two race tracks – one at Down Royal only 12 miles from Belfast, and the other at Downpatrick, a long established town in the heart of County Down which legend has it was the birthplace of Ireland's patron saint, St. Patrick.

Down Royal has claims to being one of the oldest racecourse executives in the British isles for the Down Royal Corporation of Horsebreeders was funded by Royal Charter by James II in 1685 at a course near Downpatrick and the corporation then moved in 1789 to the present site at the Maze, a small village whose name would later become associated with the Province's best known high security prison.

However, when you mentioned "The Maze" before 'The Troubles' began, there was no doubt you were talking about the racetrack where over the years much of the pomp and circumstance you would expect to see at Royal Ascot was very much part of the scene.

Up until the Seventies the Governor of Northern Ireland would, as a matter of tradition, drive along the course shortly after he arrived, usually about half-way through the meeting, and specially dressed attendants in the livery of a bygone age would play a major role in the ceremony.

All that changed after 1969. But the thread of racing continued thanks mainly to the efforts of those on the Down Royal and Downpatrick committees who kept the sport alive but more especially, I feel, to the officials of the Turf Club, then based in Dublin, who insisted on travelling North even at the height of the unrest.

The Turf Club is the Authority over racing throughout Ireland's geographic 32 counties and their officials had to be at the two Ulster tracks to keep them legal. It would have been easy for the Turf Club men to have pulled the plug but if they had done so, who knows what might have happened to trainers like George Dunwoody and others.

However, to their eternal credit men like George Walsh, now retired as Clerk of the Scales and Martin Kelly, the Clerk of the Course, stuck to their task and, along with course registrar Barry Ross – at one time manager of both Northern tracks – they kept racing in full operation when it would have been easier to close.

The one real setback came in 1971 when the labour force from Dublin, who manned the Tote, refused to travel and ever since then there has been no "official" Tote in operation at either Ulster track, although recently there has been a private one provided by the Sean Graham bookmaking organisation.

The perverse nature of the civil unrest can best be gauged by an incident which happened in October, 1971. I was preparing to travel to Longchamp to watch Mill Reef's bid for the Prix de l'Arc de Triomphe, which, of course, he duly won when into the *Belfast Telegraph* office dashed the Secretary of the Northern Ireland Bookmakers Association, Arthur McDonnell. His concern was that the Saturday meeting at Downpatrick wouldn't go ahead, apparently because of its association with the Army Benevolent Fund. This link had begun in the mists of time and no one had ever noticed it up to then. But in 1971 all liaisons were scrutinised closely by men of certain persuasion and someone had decided that Downpatrick shouldn't be supporting the Army (that is the British Army).

It looked a bit tricky for a while but common

sense prevailed eventually. The Army link was dropped and racing continued at the County Down course with, wisely, no military or political links whatsoever.

However, this didn't prevent a bomb attack on the Grandstand in 1972. Fortunately, though, the town of Downpatrick is quite simply racing mad and *all* sections of the community got together to make it clear to the men of violence that racing should be allowed to carry on unhampered.

The mood of the community appeared to get home to those who had been responsible for an isolated attack – and there was no repeat. I used to wonder whether that particular bombing incident stemmed from guys who had backed a few losers and were just making their feelings felt! You never could be sure in Northern Ireland in those days!

The trainers at that time played an outstanding role in keeping the two Northern Ireland tracks in operation.

Despite the daily reports of doom and gloom which emanated from Belfast, Southern trainers like Paddy ('Darkie') Prendergast and his son Kevin, Vincent O'Brien, Ted Curtin, Francis Flood and in later years Dermot Weld, to name but a few maintained strong support. If they hadn't done so, the two tracks couldn't have continued, depending on Northern Ireland-trained horses only.

On reflection, what was most amazing about that period, was the contrast between what was happening in Belfast and the other centres of civil strife and the way racing continued normally at Down Royal and Downpatrick. For example, the Ulster Harp Derby, the richest race in Northern Ireland, run at Down Royal, managed to attract large crowds – from all sections of the community.

It was in keeping with Irish traditions going back to the Twenties – racing remained above and beyond everything. It was the great leveller and the racecourse was the place where all men were equal and could happily rub shoulders together, unconcerned about other matters.

Racing by its very nature drew all strands of society together in a way that few other sports managed. Sectarianism was and still is totally unheard of on the Irish racing scene – North or South – and what's more, political affiliations just don't register. I have seen men of Loyalist persuasion at Irish racetracks socialising – and in many cases travelling to meetings – with those of a Nationalist viewpoint. In fact, racing still is to a large extent one great melting pot and that too in a way has preserved the sanity of many in Northern Ireland, who might otherwise have been tempted to throw in the towel during those dark days of 20 years ago.

But 'The Troubles' did create certain problems for Northern Ireland trainers like George Dunwoody, especially when it came to aiming their charges at races in the South. Delays at the Border, with checkpoints everywhere, were some things they had to learn to live with.

Dunwoody told me on one occasion: "You just couldn't move horses around at times and if you had a runner in the South of Ireland at one of the more distant tracks you had to make sure you gave yourself plenty of time."

Nowadays the whole process of travelling North and South has become much slicker with security points more sophisticated and since the beginning of 1993 there have been no Customs restrictions.

But it was a lot different back in the early Seventies, when racing was like a major adventure.

From childhood then, the hinge of Fate or Destiny – call it what you will – was operating through circumstance and through people in smoothing Richard Dunwoody's path towards the inevitable goal that would in time see him become Britain's National Hunt champion jockey.

No mention of George Dunwoody's early days can however be complete without reference to the Catherwoods, from Doagh, Co. Antrim, Stewart and Adair, who have for a long time had a lot of high class horses running in England. They were also, indirectly, to have a marked influence on young Richard's future.

In the Sixties they were heavily involved with the horses of George Dunwoody before becoming associated with the stable of Gordon Richards at Penrith from where they sent out one of the 'characters' of racing, the enigmatic Little Bay. They are still, incidentally, to this day steeped in the racing game.

"If it hadn't been for us there would have been no Richard Dunwoody," Adair told me. "We introduced George and Gillian at Punchestown and afterwards they used to join the racing set for parties at our home near Ballyclare.

"Those were great days which we'll probably not see again. I got to know Gillian through a mutual friend, Jacqueline Ward, who at that time was married to jockey Liam Ward. George I had known for some time, and in fact he used to train a lot of horses for me, including one called Solar Lady who had a lot of success in the point to point field.

"Anyway, with the social set we had at that time George and Gillian were bound to meet up and they eventually married with Stewart's brother Harry acting as Best Man.

"There was, however, one minor hiccup before then, when they broke up and didn't see each other for a time. We then travelled to Cheltenham and saw that George was so miserable we just had to ring up Gillian and ask her to come to the meeting to make up again with George, which she promptly did, so all was well!"

On the racing side Dunwoody was highly successful with a Catherwood horse called Arbuoy who won 13 times including a victory at the Punchestown Festival meeting.

Pappa Threeways was another multiple winner trained by Dunwoody for the Catherwoods who in more recent years have been associated not only with Little Bay but the ill-fated Dark Ivy who was killed in the 1987 Grand National.

A man who well remembers those Dunwoody days of the early Sixties is Billy Patton, now one of Northern Ireland's best known jump trainers but who in his younger days was a leading amateur rider with a lot of point to point successes to his name.

"George Dunwoody rode Pappa Threeways on most occasions," Billy told me, "and in fact he beat me in a Down Royal bumper one day when I thought I was on a good thing."

Billy also rode for George Dunwoody and this period coincided with the time when George arrived in County Antrim from Monaghan.

Billy's introduction to him was unusual to say

34

the least.

"The Minister of the local Ballynure Presbyterian Church called me one day and told me that a new member of his congregation was coming from Monaghan," Billy said. "The Minister said that I was the only person in the area likely to know him as he was involved in racing. So I was asked – and maybe ordered – to take George to church the first Sunday after he arrived. And so we went through the door of the vestibule, two rogues together!"

Billy added that in his view George Dunwoody was the most meticulous trainer he had ever met.

"His stables were spotless and his horses were bedded deep in straw. I have never seen a man pay more attention to detail," he told me.

Little Champ and Snow Finch were two of the most successful Dunwoody horses which Patton rode, with wins coming at Down Royal and in a number of point to points.

"Of course, George wasn't married in those days," Billy added, "and it wasn't until he left the Ballyclare area for Comber that Richard came on the scene. I have no recollection of him growing up."

The Catherwoods were the main suppliers of Dunwoody "ammunition" in those days with George turning out a lot of winners and as will be seen to be the case with Terry Casey, the wheel has since turned the full circle with George's son Richard now riding occasionally for the Catherwoods. He won on the 1990 Scottish National winner Four Trix, at Stratford on the last day of the 1991/92 season and also rode Four Trix in the 1992 Galway Plate but finished down the field.

The Catherwoods have long been major supporters of racing in Ireland North and South with Dundalk's Bunny Cox training many of their winners including Dark Ivy in the early days.

There are in fact bitter sweet memories of this horse for back in 1984 he finished third in a high class three horse race over fences at Navan. This race saw the fencing debut of Dawn Run who won followed by Buck House and Dark Ivy. All died prematurely at the height of illustrious careers.

Most of the Catherwood horses are now trained by Gordon Richards and Little Bay was arguably the one best known to the public. This was because he was such a character who ran like a champion one day and then didn't appear to want to know the next. I always associate him with Liverpool where he won three times at the National meeting with the Catherwoods and myself cheering him on each time.

That was in the early eighties but ten years later the Catherwoods are still figuring in the top echelons of the racing game and it is possible that the talents of Richard Dunwoody will help to keep them in the driving seat.

Let's now pick up the thread again with Terry Casey and we can see that his own close link with the Dunwoodys was never far away.

When Terry moved from Ireland to England, he had a spell initially at Leicester with Frank Gillman and rode the subsequent Grand National winner, Grittar to three hurdle wins before returning to Northern Ireland to help Archie Watson when the Armagh trainer fell ill. He also spent some time as Head Man with Paddy Mullins at Goresbridge in

County Kilkenny. Then in 1984 he took out a trainer's licence and trained for two years at the Curragh.

Casey decided to leave again for England late in 1985 and trained for John Upson at Towcester. It was at this time that Richard Dunwoody was beginning to hit the headlines. After West Tip's fall at Bechers in the 1985 Grand National, Dunwoody was grimly determined to make up for this misfortune in the 1986 renewal.

Before the National of that year, however, he was engaged to ride a horse in what was known for years as the Topham Trophy on the first day of the meeting. And the horse in question was trained by one Terry Casey.

The horse was Glen Rue, Dunwoody's first mount for Casey, and he duly trotted up at 20/1 to provide a fairytale reunion and gave myself and colleague Ray Glennon a nice contribution towards the expenses at Aintree, for we were tipped off beforehand.

"I knew then I'd win the National," recalled Richard. "I regarded the Topham as an omen and it was wonderful to score for Terry after all those years."

"One of the greatest days of my life," Terry Casey told me. "You know later in the 1987-88 season I had second claim on Richard after David Nicholson. He rode 16 winners for me then. Now and again I like to bring out the old contract just to look at it. It's difficult sometimes taking in the fact that this man, now at the very top of his profession, used to ride and win on a regular basis for a humble man from Donegal."

As we shall see in the next chapter, it was in

1972 that Richard Dunwoody moved to England as an eight-year-old, with the family and by a strange coincidence, it was that same year that John Reid also left his native Northern Ireland – though he was seventeen at the time and had a Flat career which took off in a way he could never have imagined. For Reid, of course, went on to win the Epsom Derby on Dr Devious (1992), the Prix de l'Arc de Triomphe on Tony Binn (1988), the Irish Derby on Sir Harry Lewis (1987) and the King George VI and Queen Elizabeth Stakes on Ile de Bourbon (1978) among many major successes.

And another Northern Ireland-born jockey, Ray Cochrane would also make it "big" in England, winning the Epsom Derby on Kahyasi for Luca Cumani and the Aga Khan in 1988 and following up by winning the Irish Derby on the same colt.

So Northern Ireland could justly lay claim to producing the "goods" when it came to jockeys of outstanding talent. And of this trio the one with the greatest talent of all was unquestionably Richard Dunwoody, though whether comparisons should be drawn between Flat and National Hunt jockeys is a debatable point.

The late Sean Graham, a pioneer of the book-making profession, who was fearless as a rails bookie and who set standards always for others to follow, loved nothing better than to spot a star-in-the-making, especially from his own Province.

"That boy will be a champion one day," he said of Dunwoody before the racing world had really awakened to his talent.

Sadly, Graham did not live to see his prediction realised. But he did manage to etch in his mind the picture of Richard Dunwoody winning the 1986

Aintree Grand National.

Two days after the running of that race Sean Graham died in hospital from the terminal illness with which he had battled so courageously for so long.

CHAPTER 4

THE MOVE TO ENGLAND

George Dunwoody, wife Gillian and the eight-year-old Richard left Northern Ireland in 1972 when Gillian's mother, who still lived in England, became ill.

"My wife is an only child and when her mother became unwell I realised this was the time to break with home and travel back with Jill," George said. "Of course, I had a lot of regrets leaving Northern Ireland and felt I would miss the many friendships I had established over the years, but at the end of the day it proved to be a wise decision. Richard would not have become the jockey he is, based in Northern Ireland. That goes without saying."

George had applied for a job with an American who was attempting to convert a cattle farm into a stud farm in Gloucester and to his delight – and no doubt relief – George was soon appointed manager.

"I had 200 acres to fence in and I worked for a man named William Reynolds who gave me a free hand," George said. "With racing very much in my blood I was delighted to be associated with such an undertaking and there was a lot of class about the mares that Mr. Reynolds kept.

"But if the horses were bred in the purple, what about our new neighbour? It was not long after I

41

had moved that Prince Charles bought Highgrove next door to us although I never saw him during the five years I was there."

While George was earning the cash for the family to live on, the young Dunwoody was attending boarding school at Rencombe College between Cirencester and Cheltenham but, more importantly from a racing point of view, he hadn't lost his interest in horse riding and in fact Tony the pony had travelled from Ulster with him.

"When Richard came home on holidays he would renew his acquaintance with Tony," George told me, "and he also went hunting with the Beaufort Pony Club. However, much to my regret we had to leave Charltondown because the owner's wife wanted to go back to America and Mr. Reynolds eventually sold the farm so I became redundant.

"Still, I was a racing man and I knew many people in the game so I wasn't too disheartened. I was nearing retiring age anyway so I decided to move closer to the centre of the action in Newmarket although Richard stayed at Rencombe College. I bought a home in Newmarket and among the first to come and visit me was Paul Kelleway who told me he had heard I was in town and asked me if I was interested in riding out for him.

"I jumped at the chance. Richard came too during the school breaks so that this was the first time he was given the opportunity to ride thoroughbreds.

"Richard was only 13 at the time and soon began riding out two year olds and three year olds for Paul who was delighted with his style."

"I taught him all he knows," joked Kelleway

when I talked to him about the young Dunwoody. "He used to come here during the school holidays when his father was riding out for me and on the mornings he was due to appear George would always say: 'The young fellow will be here today. Look after him.'

"I can't remember where I first met George for I was only in Ireland twice in my life! Perhaps it was at Tattersalls Sales at Newmarket before George came to live in the town. Anyway, he was very soon riding out for me and we struck up a close friendship.

"It was obvious when I first saw Richard that he had been well taught in the art of riding horses and I felt I could put him up on anything without any worries. You know, it used to be the case in some yards that a lad was rarely if ever given a chance to ride decent horses when only in his early teens as was the case with Dunwoody. But I never believed in that. I wanted to give him a chance.

"Even though he was only riding out for me to pass the time between school terms, it was obvious that he wanted to be a jockey for he wasn't all that keen on eating! I used to think that perhaps he was a bit anorexic. He certainly wasn't as tough as he later became. In fact, he looked a bit puny.

"But at that time he was dreaming about being a Flat jockey. The National Hunt game wasn't featuring in his mind so perhaps he felt he had to keep his weight down, even though he was only 13 years old!"

George and Richard Dunwoody became a regular team during those summers of the late Seventies and early Eighties and some of the horses which Richard rode out went on to greater things.

Donegal Prince was probably the best of them for he won the 1981 Chester Cup and the Queen Alexandra Stakes at Royal Ascot, in addition to scoring in the Tote Gold Trophy Hurdle at Newbury on one of the few occasions when it wasn't abandoned because of frost in those days.

Kelleway reckons that Richard rode Donegal Prince as much as anyone during the summer of 1980 before the gelding went on to his triumphs the following spring and summer. Then in February 1982 when Dunwoody had already begun his career in racing and left the Kelleway stable, Donegal Prince took the Tote Gold Trophy with John Francome doing the honours.

It was while Dunwoody was making those fleeting summer visits to the Kelleway yard that another young jockey – or jockette – was also taking her first strides in the racing game. Kelleway's daughter Gaye, who was later to blossom into one of England's finest pilots, landed her first winner on a horse called Sass at Newmarket on August 1, 1981 – and Richard Dunwoody was there to lead the winner in.

"It wasn't because he was associated with the horse in any manner for he didn't have a job with me," Paul said. "I feel he just wanted to be there because it was such a special occasion for Gaye." Although some of the gilt was taken from the gingerbread when the young Kelleway was stood down for excessive use of the whip.

"Imagine that. Her first win and she fell foul of the Stewards," Paul said. "Still, it was a memorable occasion, but to be honest I can't remember Richard leading Gaye in.

"It wasn't until I was looking at the picture of the lead in at my home in Spain that I noticed it was Richard and immediately I showed it to my wife. It just hadn't registered with the passing of time. From those far off days when Richard was only 17 to the heady days of champion jockey. Time certainly passes quickly at this game."

Richard later rode for Kelleway when he eventually became established and even after he had won the title he was still keeping in contact with the odd phone call or two.

"You know, I regard Dunwoody as a phenomenon like Willie Carson," Kelleway said. "For years he was just around and really didn't do a lot. Then he suddenly blossomed and now he is at the top. I view him as a late developer, for although I saw that he was keen enough to be a jockey when he was around my place, I would never have tipped him as a future champion. Not on your life. He just lacked that hard cutting edge which champions appear to be born with.

"It's a different matter nowadays, isn't it?"

Richard doesn't quite register with Kelleway in the manner of another Irish jockey Ronnie Beggan, who was responsible for landing one of the great Cheltenham coups when taking the Sun Alliance Novices Chase on Asir in 1985. Paul would much rather talk about that day.

"I must have won £100,000 on that horse," Paul said gleefully as he recalled a race indelibly imprinted on his mind. "I remember David Mould came up to me and asked me 'Where did you get that jockey?' I told him 'from out of the clouds'!"

The Dunwoody association with Kelleway eventually came to an end in the late summer of 1981 when George decided to move on and Richard had come to a major crossroads in what was by now a packed life.

Racing versus an academic career became very much a priority in the Dunwoody household as Richard proved to be successful at school beyond his parents' wildest dreams. He achieved 10 'O' Levels and seemed set for a career outside the Turf. But the old bug was still there.

Eventually, Richard's mother asked an old friend John Bosley, who trained near Bampton in Oxfordshire, if he would take Richard on when the lad had left school and "knock this racing non-sense out of his head."

Bosley had ridden for Gillian's father, Dick and not only that, had ridden a few winners. So it was no big deal taking on the young Dunwoody and seeing what he was made of.

"Richard joined my small stable at the end of August 1981, straight from school and began to ride out for me as well as looking after some of my horses," John said. "I hadn't many in the stable but Richard played his part and was lucky enough to be in charge of a two year old named Corn Street. He took it to Wolverhampton for its first outing and it duly won.

"Richard used to school horses over fences for me as well and I'll never forget the first time I saw him in action. It was soon plain to me that although he had show jumped he had never really schooled a racehorse before – and he fell off. Well, he had a false front tooth then and the tooth fell out.

"Later we went in and had lunch but afterwards young Richard spent about another three hours searching the schooling paddock and going through every blade of grass before he eventually found that tooth. He certainly wasn't going to buy a new one.

"Richard was also friendly with my son who was close to his age and they later celebrated a joint 21st birthday party. Martin – later to be Dunwoody's best man – is also a jockey but not in the Dunwoody class, although like myself he still has happy memories of those early days.

"Richard was only with me until December 1981, a period of four months, but during that time I knew he was heading for the top and that my small stable would be of no further use to him."

The time had come for a change in the Dunwoody career and George Dunwoody felt that his son should now join a top flight stable where Richard would receive the best education possible in the art of riding winners.

"I chose Captain Tim Forster at Letcombe Bassett because he had a tremendous reputation but, more important even than that, a good friend of mine from Ulster, Captain Dick Ker, who is a steward at Newbury, was acquainted with Forster and agreed to put in a kind word."

Dick Ker bred horses for the Flat at Donaghadee on the County Down coast, so he wasn't far from the Dunwoody stables at Carrowdore during the late Sixties. However he had known George for much longer than that.

"We met when we became regulars at the point to points," he told me. "I was heavily involved in racing at that time and in fact I am still a member of the Irish National Hunt Steeplechase Committee.

"When George moved to Carrowdore it seemed only natural that I should give him some of my jumpers to train and we struck up a reasonably profitable partnership.

"I'll always remember a horse named Capernican which I owned and which was trained by Frankie Fitzsimmons near Downpatrick before moving to the Dunwoody yard. Capernican went on to run at Fairyhouse in a hunter chase with Ben Hanbury on board and landed a nice 'touch' for us (incidentally, the young Dunwoody later maintained the link with Hanbury – now a trainer – by riding out for Ben, a family friend in 1977).

"I had very few jumpers around the place for I concentrated on the Flat and in this respect I have happy memories of a mare, Floral Star, given to me by my father. She went on to foal the first winner I ever bred on the English scene, Shipwreck by Pandemonium. Shipwreck was trained by Arthur Budgett to win a small race at Warwick."

During those days at Donaghadee, Captain Ker got to know the young Dunwoody through the North Down Pony Club which Richard had joined at an early age. "My wife and I used to run the pony camps and Richard would come along," Ker said. "Even in those days he showed that flair for horses which he has never lost."

The Kers eventually left Donaghadee in 1979, seven years after the Dunwoodys, and moved to Wiltshire. "It was a family decision," Ker said. –My son was in business in London and certainly wasn't going to follow me into farming so I felt it was time to move on. I still kept in touch with George and it was when he was planning Richard's career at the end of 1981 that he gave me a call.

"He asked if I had any contacts among the trainers in England and I told him about my friendship with Captain Tim Forster who had served with the 11th Hussars in Omagh, County Tyrone back in the Sixties.

"Captain Forster and myself were in partnership with some horses so I knew him well enough to recommend the young Dunwoody. I'm glad to see his career has blossomed from those early days.

"Of course it has to be said that all sportsmen need a bit of luck and Richard's came when Hywel Davies the stable jockey with Captain Forster, was injured and Richard came in for more rides earlier than he might have expected.

"Later, when David Nicholson came calling, looking for Richard's services, Richard might have stayed with Captain Forster had he been made stable jockey but Hywel wasn't that much older than him and obviously had many years to go. In addition, the Captain remained loyal to Hywel and at the end of the day Richard had to move to Nicholson.

"He has certainly gained in strength and talent over the years and one aspect about his riding which I like is his ability to put a horse in a race with a chance at just the right time. Now that he is with Martin Pipe and all that that means in the way of ammunition, I can see him being champion for a few years yet for he seems to enjoy the daily grind.

"You know, weeks before Peter Scudamore made his announcement to call it a day, I would have bet good money that he was going to quit. He had the look of a man who was thoroughly fed up with the treadmill life of a champion jockey and I felt he was ready to go at any time in order to try something new. It was no surprise to me when he made his feelings public.

"I can't see Dunwoody becoming disenchanted for a long time to come. That's why I feel he will stay on top, but it's a hard world, that's for sure."

So at the end of December 1981 Richard Dunwoody joined Captain Tim Forster and saw his career soar to heights from which it has never fallen.

Tim Forster was one of the old school, a man steeped in chasing who told me, "I never had a hurdler about me." Well, that was the case until the 1992-93 season when the Captain suddenly began sending out horses over hurdles and what's more, they won! Those winners were Forster's first hurdling successes but he pointed out to me that with the dearth of chasers he felt he had no option but to diversify.

"There are no horses around like Arkle and Mill House," he told me mournfully. "Do you remember the days when the Cheltenham Gold Cup had at least half a dozen top class chasers in with a chance? You don't get that nowadays, do you?"

Captain Forster also had a remarkable record in the Grand National by the time Dunwoody arrived on the scene a month before his eighteenth birthday. Up until that time the Captain, as Dunwoody still likes to call him, had landed the tradition-soaked Aintree chase twice.

Well To Do won a memorable battle with Gay Trip on the run for home in 1972 when it was all to play for from the last fence and in doing so not only gave jockey Graham Thorner his first and only National winner, he also deprived Terry Biddlecombe of a National success to make up for the fact that two years earlier he had lost the mount on Gay Trip to Pat Taaffe when Gay Trip won at 15/1 for Fred Rimell. Captain Forster's second National win followed in 1980 when Ben Nevis landed the prize with American amateur Charlie Fenwick in the saddle.

John Francome, arguably the best jockey never to have won a National, finished second on Fred Winter's Rough and Tumble with The Pilgarlic third. That was the year when only four finished the course – and there was no multiple pile-up. The National has certainly changed in a short space of time.

Forster was to win the great race again in 1985 when Dunwoody was very much a part of his stable but tail swishing Last Suspect who scored on that occasion was ridden by the stable No. 1 Hywel Davies while by then Dunwoody had begun his memorable partnership with Michael Oliver's West Tip, who fell at Bechers when looking all over the winner.

Dunwoody, then, was joining a real jumping stable in 1981 and Forster recalled: "As soon as I saw him riding out I knew he was a natural. He had an indefinable style and an empathy with a horse which was rare to find. I knew he was something special but he was young and small and I didn't want to ruin him. He was, I felt, like a young horse who had to be brought along slowly and allowed to mature."

Captain Ker was equally sure of the teenager's future and had told Forster: "I think I have seen a youngster who will make a great jockey. Will you take him on?" Forster never regretted the move for he feels that those years when Dunwoody was about his stable helped to mould the Ulsterman's career.

Forster's first step was to get Richard a point to point rider's licence for he had told his close friend Colin Nash about the new recruit and Nash had a lot of good point to pointers about him.

It turned out that Forster was too late in applying for the licence so Richard had to miss that first season. But as the Captain said: "It was all for the best for this gave Richard time to find his feet in the game. I told Colin that if he put him up on his horses he wouldn't go far wrong and it was Colin who gave Richard his first ever winner the following season, in 1983."

Before then, however, Richard had tasted the heady atmosphere of riding in a race for the first time when he rang up Welshman Dr. Arthur Jones for the mount on Mallard Song at Chepstow in August 1982 and finished second in an amateur Flat race.

"Dr. Jones was a friend of the Captain's," Richard told me, "and I just approached him for the ride out of the blue. It gave me a great thrill to finish second but my heart was on jumping and Colin Nash used to have a few horses around the Captain's yard which I schooled."

Eventually Forster and Nash were able to see what the youngster was made of for on Easter Monday, 1983 he had the leg up on Game Trust in the Old Berkshire Members Race at Lockinge point to point and the mare duly obliged. And then in early May of that same year Richard rode Game Trust again and had his first winner under rules when Game Trust scored in a novice hunter chase at Cheltenham.

"I'll never forget that mare," Richard told me. "She has a special place in my heart just like West Tip had in later years."

By now Captain Forster knew that he had something to work with in Richard Dunwoody but he was still determined not to rush him. He was fortunate, too, that Dunwoody's parents, having been in the racing game all their lives, were patient and willing to allow Forster to get on with it. "Had I pushed on with his career, he might have turned sour," Forster told me.

"Mentally he could have boiled over as so many have done at an early stage in this game and he might have ended up in a muddle. He was too gifted for me to allow that to happen."

Dunwoody eventually got his chances on Forster's horses and it wasn't long before his first winner turned out by the Captain came along.

"I had been impressed by his win on Game Trust so I put him up on a difficult horse called Swordsman at Fontwell on May 30, 1983," Forster said. "I told the owner that Dunwoody had talent and to trust me although I knew that Swordsman was a difficult ride. But Richard rode the horse superbly."

Swordsman won that race by four lengths, beating Spinning Saint and Cruise Missile and later in this career, the following season in fact, Dunwoody was to become re-acquainted with Spinning Saint on a day which has passed into racing folklore.

In March 1984 at Hereford, Dunwoody, now making the headlines as an amateur rider with the winning habit, was booked to ride in all seven races for the first time in his life.

"At that time all my jockeys were injured and I had no one to ride Toy Track who was a big battler of a horse," said Forster. "To be honest, I didn't think Richard could handle him and I thought I was sending a lamb to the slaughter. Then when I heard that he had rides with other stables which meant he would be racing all day, I couldn't sleep for I thought Richard would die from exhaustion!"

Well, the Captain needn't have worried for Toy Track, who was running in a novice chase – what else! jumped off with the leaders and Dunwoody brought him home first to land a leg of a four-timer which is still talked about in the Forster yard.

Richard in fact had three mounts for the Captain and the others finished second and third. He might even have had a five-timer, as he was only beaten a neck on Forster's Mr. Bee in the last race.

Spinning Saint was also one of his successes. At that time he was trained by Kim Bailey at Lambourn and the other two wins were supplied by Bob Champion with Three Chances and Mrs. Doreen Tucker with Pucka Fella.

That Hereford four-timer brought 20-years-old Dunwoody a blaze of publicity and it was now obvious to everyone outside the Forster yard that here was a new force on the racing scene, one who might even replace John Francome who was easing out from race riding around that time.

The season 1983-84 saw Dunwoody finish up third behind Simon Sherwood and Dermot Browne in the amateur riders championship with 24 winners from 211 rides and shortly afterwards he turned professional.

However, 1983-84 was memorable for another

THOSE DESSIE DAYS

Desert Orchid going to the start for the 1990 Cheltenham Gold Cup in which he finished third. Watching him (on right) is owner Richard Burridge (the taller). Picture: Bernard Parkin.

*Desert Orchid (top) makes a mistake at the second last, handing th
advantage to Norton's Coin (right) in the 1990 Gold Cup and (below
Toby Tobias (Mark Pitman) the runner-up (on inside) jumping the las
with eventual winner Norton's Coin (Graham McCourt) with Deser
Orchid (Richard Dunwoody) rising to the fence and (inset) Sirre*
Griffiths, owner-trainer of Norton's Coin with Gold Cup.

Trainer David Elsworth (top) being presented with his trophy by the Queen Mother after the 1989 Gold Cup and (below) Yahoo (Tom Morgan) looks to be in command at the last but Desert Orchid (Simon Sherwood) came out on top in a memorable battle up the hill.

Desert Orchid powering to what looked like an easy victory in the 1990 Jameson Irish Grand National until the grey made a dreadful mistake at the last (bottom) and Richard Dunwoody did very well to remain in the saddle and, surviving the moment of crisis, went on to win by twelve lengths.

Desert Orchid (top) in one of his greatest triumphs, taking the Racing Post Handicap Chase under 12-3 at Kempton in February, 1990 and (below) how his legion of fans like to remember him, Caroline Norris's picture of the cap at a jaunty angle on his head as Janice Coyle leads him round in the winner's enclosure to the acclaim of the dense crowd after the 1989 Gold Cup.

David 'The Duke' Nicholson after Charter Party (Richard Dunwoody), right, had won the 1988 Gold Cup and (below) Dunwoody safely negotiates the last before going on for a six-lengths victory.

Richard Dunwoody's "crowning glory", according to 'The Duke' Nicholson, when he won the 1989 Arkle Challenge Trophy (top) on Waterloo Boy and (below), left, locked in battle with Barnbrook Again (Hywel Davies) in the epic battle for the 1990 Queen Mother Champion Chase, followed by Sabin Du Loir (Peter Scudamore, right) and Feroda (Tom Taaffe) behind. Waterloo Boy lost this one by half-a-length.

Ed Byrne's magnificent study of Remittance Man and Richard Dunwoody (top) winning at Newbury and (below) Jamie Osborne has the mount on Remittance Man (centre), as he wins an unforgettable contest for the Queen Mother Champion Chase at the 1992 Festival meeting from Katabatic (Simon McNeill), left and Waterloo Boy (Richard Dunwoody), right.

reason. A horse called West Tip.

Richard had begun taking spare mounts from Droitwich trainer Michael Oliver and in March of 1984 he was asked to ride West Tip in the Midlands Grand National.

West Tip was a horse who shouldn't have been fit to race at all. For early in his career while out doing road work he was struck by an articulated lorry and received a horrendous injury which almost ripped out his hindquarter.

Happily he recovered so that by the time the young amateur Dunwoody was engaged to ride him in April 1984 he was a novice chaser with a future.

West Tip had won at Wolverhampton and Haydock and been placed on five other occasions that season, notably when beaten two-and-a-half lengths by A Kinsman in the Fred Withington Chase at Cheltenham. He had also gone down by 10 lengths to Ballinacurra Lad in the Embassy Premier Chase Final at Ascot, so by the time Dunwoody came along he had established an encouraging reputation.

But there was no fairytale start to the new partnership, for West Tip finished ninth behind Mr. Mole in the big Uttoxeter race and Dunwoody later told me: "He just would not act on the firm ground, although I knew he would be a good class staying chaser with some give underfoot."

Dunwoody always gives his horses time. Even though he was beaten again on West Tip the following season – he had turned professional by then – he knew there were better days ahead, and they weren't long coming round as far as West Tip and himself were concerned. But before West Tip and Dunwoody registered their first win together Richard had taken a major step up the ladder with a win on a gelding trained in a tiny stable in St. Austell in Cornwall. Graham Roach was the name of the trainer and the horse was Prideaux Boy.

"I rode Prideaux Boy in the Mecca Hurdle at Sandown in December that year and this was the win which gave me the breakthrough," Richard asserted.

Why? "Well, it was on television for one thing and for another it brought about those phone calls asking me to take rides for other stables. At that time I was riding No. 2 to Hywel Davies for Captain Forster and I was keen to make my mark quickly."

Prideaux Boy had won at Wincanton in November 1984 and looked like doing so again later that month but he came down when in second place.

Roach decided to run him again at Sandown and looked around for a jockey he felt might continue the winning sequence. "I saw Dunwoody riding and I thought he had great style and rapport with a horse," Roach said. "In fact, he reminded me even in those days of Francome and Jonjo. I was friendly with his agent and booked him for Prideaux Boy, although I was in Hungary on holiday at the time and didn't see the race.

"My wife and friends brought the horse up to Sandown. I was a permit holder and Prideaux Boy was one of the first horses I had bought. He was more than useful for he turned into a good chaser as well and I'm sorry I didn't see him win that day. But I must tell you my experience on the afternoon of Prideaux Boy's success.

"We were in a hotel on the Romanian border and a friend came down the stairs to tell me he had heard on the BBC World Service that Prideaux Boy had won. I couldn't believe it and promptly celebrated with some Russian champagne. It was awful stuff, but who cared?"

Prideaux Boy's win at Sandown was just over two weeks after his fall at Wincanton and he was none the worse for that setback. He took up the running from Rushmoor two out but the latter rallied strongly and Dunwoody had to use all his skills to keep Prideaux Boy at his work and draw away in the run in to win by five lengths from Rushmoor who was disqualified and moved down a place for hampering the third horse.

Dunwoody was now on his way and it wasn't long before West Tip loomed up again. Michael Oliver's gelding was being trained for the National that season and an ideal prep race was the Mildmay-Cazalet Chase at Sandown in January. West Tip duly obliged but only because of the superb skill executed by Dunwoody who got him home by a length from the top weight Canny Danny.

It had become obvious that West Tip wasn't an easy ride for he wold drop his bit given half a chance. The result was that when the race was run at a slow pace and then quickened a jockey had to be ready to get West Tip going quickly. Dunwoody was up to this and more. Driven along from a long way out West Tip gradually wore down the leader and Dunwoody came in knowing he might just have a future National winner on his hands.

Better was to come for later that month West Tip went to Cheltenham for the Holsten Distributors

Chase and in another slowly run race was left behind when the pace suddenly quickened. However, again Dunwoody was up to the occasion and he rallied his partner to catch Door Latch near the line. That same Door Latch who was bred by his good friend Jimmy Burgess from his days in County Down.

After the publication of the National weights West Tip won two more races – at Hereford and Cheltenham, the latter the Ritz Club Trophy at the Festival meeting where Dunwoody was also successful on the stablemate Von Trappe in the Coral golden Hurdle Final.

Dunwoody really shone in the Ritz Club and so did West Tip as he threaded his way through into the lead just after the last and ran on strongly to beat Acarine by four lengths. The horse obviously had the right credentials for the National. He was in great form, he stayed well, jumped soundly and had less weight than he deserved. He looked a certainty – but Bechers caught him out.

Second time around at Bechers, the 22nd fence, has proved the downfall of more than one National contender. So near and yet so far. The second circuit with all to play for and you enter the area where quite a number of the field will either have fallen or retired.

There is no better feeling for a jockey than to be on a horse still cantering at the head of affairs with the race seemingly at his mercy.

This was the case with West Tip in the 1985 National but the fate which had struck five times in the previous 10 years was to pounce again.

Golden Rapper, going well in 1976, crashed here; so did Andy Pandy who must have deprived

Red Rum of his third national in 1977; Gold Cup winner Alverton was fatally injured here in 1979; Delmoss went down in 1980 and Pacify the following year. Then it was the turn of West Tip.

Co-favourite at 13/2 West Tip had gone smoothly from the start and was swinging along on the bridle along with Rupertino and Corbiere as he approached the fence.

Then it happened. West Tip seemed to lose his landing gear and down he went with Dunwoody ending up in a disappointed crumpled heap.

"I could have cried," he told me. "Obviously I was going so well and although there was still someway to go he must surely have won that year. I could only sit there and watch the rest of the field thunder past. Frustrating? You've no idea!"

The irony of it all was that in one of the best finishes for years, Last Suspect, the 50/1 chance, came through to win for – guess who? Tim Forster and Hywel Davies.

Davies had pleaded with the Captain to run the horse which appeared, on the book, to have no chance.

But once again those famous colours of Anne Duchess of Westminster appeared at the sharp end of a major race and Last Suspect went in as one of the least fancied National winners of the last 20 years.

Dunwoody had every reason to feel despondent. But he's no fool. He knew his turn would come. And it came with a vengeance in 1986. Before then Dunwoody had the satisfaction of knowing that he had knocked up 46 winners in his first season as a professional to put himself into joint seventh place behind John Francome, who by coincidence had just bowed out.

With Francome out of the jockey's championship – many thought at a premature age – the centre of attention focussed on Francome's close friend Peter Scudamore who was riding No. 1 for David Nicholson and appeared to be the man they all had to beat for the championship. Dunwoody was now riding No. 2 with Nicholson and was still attached to Tim Forster, although the Letcombe Bassett trainer still had Davies as his No. 1. A lot of chances then for Dunwoody to make a name for himself and go far in the race for the title, but closer to his heart was the National, the race every jump jockey wanted to win.

After West Tip's disaster at Becher's second time round, the public and the Press rolled in behind his chances the following year and I felt at the time he was sure to start a very hot favourite.

I remember chatting to Dunwoody at the end of 1985 and he told me that West Tip was the one they all had to beat.

I promptly told the BBC Northern Ireland television audience and did myself a major favour in the process.

CHAPTER 5

THE CAPTAIN ACTS THE GENTLEMAN!

Richard Dunwoody might have missed the winning ride on West Tip in the 1986 Aintree Grand National had Captain Tim Forster not acted like a total gentleman.

Dunwoody was earmarked by Captain Forster to ride Port Askaig for Lord Chelsea. After all, he had first claim on Richard and no one could blame him for exercising it.

The irony of it was that for a time that season Dunwoody had reason to surmise that Port Askaig might be a better National proposition at the end of the day than West Tip. Granted, he was not every rider's cup of tea as earlier in his career he had been prone to make mistakes.

However, wearing blinkers, he had become an improved character and finished an excellent second, beaten only three-quarters-of-a-length by Knock Hill in the Brooke Bond Oxo National (4m 1f) at Warwick in January of '86. And he was well clear of the remainder of the field when going down by only one and a half lengths over three miles to the subsequent National winner, Maori Venture (1987) at Lingfield in March. With Dunwoody in the saddle he was staying on well over the last three fences under strong driving.

In contrast, West Tip, although he had shone the previous season, had failed to score in the 1985-'86 season – before the National weights were published on January 30. Out of five starts his best performance was a half a length second to Burrough Hill Lad, the 1984 Gold Cup winner, in the Rehearsal Chase at Chepstow, on November 20 , but this was a tremendous performance, for the event wasn't a handicap!.

Dunwoody wasn't completely sold on West Tip until Newbury the month before the Aintree race when he jumped well and displayed excellent stamina carrying top weight (11st 7lbs) to a 2½-lengths victory over the smart Beau Ranger. It was after this race that Dunwoody went to Captain Forster and asked to be allowed to switch.

"Well, what could I do," said the urbane Forster, adding with tongue in cheek: "I am a gentleman and the kindest trainer in the country! Of course, I agreed to help Richard."

On a more serious note, he went on to state that the real facts of the matter were that he realised that the Michael Oliver-trained West Tip had a much better chance in the race than Port Askaig and it would have been churlish of him to have prevented Richard taking the ride.

So Graham McCourt became Port Askaig's rider on the day and Lord Chelsea's gelding fell at the first. That , as they say, is life.

West Tip, a nine-year-old, which many experts regarded as the ideal age for a potential National winner, was given 10st 8lbs which later became 10st 11lbs with the general rise in the handicap. He was joint favourite in most ante-post lists and there was little doubt that in the judgement of shrewd punters, he was one who simply could not be left out of the reckoning and would take all the beating off his handicap mark.

On the day of the race itself he would go off at 15/2, the favourite at 13/2 being Mr. Snugfit, the 1985 runner-up, owned by the colourful Terry Ramsden.

Ramsden, one of the heaviest "players" of all in the ring at that time, had gone for a massive killing both in single bets and in doubles and trebles. He had £50,000 each way on Mr. Snugfit at 8/1 and was terribly unlucky not to have collected on the place bet as 'Snugfit', responding to pressure from the third last finished fastest of all and would have been third in another stride (Classified denied him third place by half-a-length).

He doubled Mr. Snugfit, incidentally, with two horses of his own, Stearsby which won the Whitbread Best Mild Novices Chase on the Thursday at 11/4 and Brunico, third in the Glenlivet Hurdle on the Friday, starting 7/4 favourite and he also had trebles coupling all three.

Dunwoody got the perfect confidence booster on the Thursday of the Liverpool meeting when partnering Glenrue for Terry Casey to that neck victory over Bright Oasis in the Whitbread Trophy Handicap Chase, going clear after jumping Becher's and, after shaking off the challenge of Preben Star at the second last, withstanding the late run of Bright Oasis for whom the post came just too soon.

You could see on Dunwoody's face after that success the look of a man who was riding with destiny. And when a sprinkling of snow fell to ease the ground the night before the race, the script for

West Tip's success was now in final draft form.

For the first time since the Sixties there were three previous winners of the race, one of them the formidable Corbiere, winner in 1983 and still a threat in subsequent years with third places to Hallo Dandy in 1984 and Last Suspect in 1985.

The withdrawal of Burrough Hill Lad (12st), Combs Ditch (11st 11lbs), Galway Blaze (11st 5lbs) and Run and Skip (11st 5lbs) left Corbiere at the top of the weights carrying 11st 7lbs.

The automatic top weight in the race, the Czech horse Essex had 12 stone but this was because he hadn't been handicapped in England.

Door Latch (9/1) went at the first with Port Askaig, then the gallant Corbiere uncharacteristically fell at the fourth and soon it was Doubleyouagain, Kilkilowen, Tacroy and Essex who took them along.

At Becher's first time it was Tacroy slightly in the lead from Doubleyouagain, Tacroy, Essex, Kilkilowen and The Tsarevitch and at the Canal Turn it was much the same order.

At Valentines, where there was little change in the leaders, West Tip was lobbing along in eighth place and running well within himself, although Dunwoody received a bit of a fright when West Tip got a bit close to The Tsarevitch at the Chair and didn't jump too well.

However, he was soon back into his rhythm and on the second circuit he tracked the leaders who by this time were Kilkilowen, The Tsarevitch and Classified, beautifully placed on the outside and ready to pounce. No mistakes this time as the field went on to the Canal Turn where the Irish hope, Monanore, trained in County Tipperary by Bill

Harney and ridden by Tom Morgan, had made up ground from the rear and was disputing the lead along with Young Driver.

Over Anchor Bridge crossing and Monanore, Classified, Young Driver, Kilkilowen and the relentlessly galloping West Tip appeared to have it between them with Dunwoody in the distinctive pale blue colours with the purple sash giving the impression he was ready to take charge at any time.

Although the youngest rider in the race, Dunwoody knew he had to exercise patience for once in front West Tip was inclined to idle. So Richard left it until the Elbow – by which time Young Driver was in front – before he made his move.

West Tip looked like going clear in a matter of strides, but again he momentarily failed to go on and Dunwoody had to ride him out as Young Driver, running his heart out, battled back very gamely, indeed, and the winning distance was just two lengths.

A delighted Dunwoody said afterwards: "You never stop riding in the National."

As he sat and sipped the traditional glass of champagne at the Press Conference he didn't forget to thank Captain Forster for his help in letting him ride West Tip. And Lord Chelsea was thanked as well. Always the diplomat, our Richard . . .

Then it was on to the story of the race. "I thought he might have hit the front too soon, for he's inclined to idle when he does so, but there was really no problem," he said.

"The only doubt I had was at the Canal Turn first time when I jumped into Ten Cherries but I soon regained control and was happy to go down the inside of the track. I was fine both times at Bechers and in fact West Tip never jumped this fence as well as he did today.

"Really, the only horse I was worried about was The Tsarevitch. To me he represented the class horse in the race."

Asked when he thought he would win the race, Dunwoody replied: "At the third last. At that stage there were a number of horses going well ahead of me but I knew that I would beat them if I kept my head."

Looking back on that singular triumph later, he would tell me: "West Tip's win is still the best moment of my career, and I have won the Gold Cup and Champion Hurdle. I was totally elated afterwards. Subsequently on the occasions when I failed to complete the course twice, it made me realise how difficult it is to win this race.

"West Tip was probably the best National horse in recent years, apart from Red Rum. After all, he managed two fourths and a second after that win and he was also placed fourth in a Gold Cup and won the Ritz Club at the Festival meeting. Not many will come close to that."

Dunwoody, then, was sampling the same dizzy heights which his "stable companion" at Tim Forster's, Hywel Davies, had scaled the previous year. Davies, reckoned to be one of the strongest riders in a finish in the whole of Britain, was very definitely Forster's No. 1.

And it was of course Davies, you'll remember, who rode Barnbrook Again in that hectic nail-biting climax to the Champion Chase at Cheltenham in 1990 when Dunwoody was runner-up on

Waterloo Boy.

Hywel naturally still recalls that race as though it were yesterday. But what's more vivid is his memory of the day when he literally died to give the young Dunwoody his first stepping stone on the path to glory.

It was at Doncaster, in February, 1984 and the horse Davies was riding, Solid Rock, fell at the last fence with the jockey pinned underneath.

"I was upsides Ridley Lamb at the time and he was riding Fortina's Express: The next I knew I was on the floor and then I blacked out.

"They tell me that on the way to the hospital I was in such deep concussion that my heart stopped beating seven times because it was receiving no messages from the brain and the doctor attending had to keep bringing me back to life again with shock treatment.

"That was the darkest day of my career for I was on the way to riding 100 winners that season, for the first time."

However, Davies' injury provided Dunwoody with that window of opportunity which all sportsmen need, for with Hywel in hospital Captain Forster had to have a sound replacement – and Dunwoody was the man who was called up.

Richard was also fortunate in that the Captain's horses had ben suffering from the virus at that time and as a result they were remarkably well handicapped. So when they started to run up to form, they also started to win and Richard was there on the ground floor.

Davies' earliest memory of the young Dunwoody is of the teenager riding out and taking part in the usual stable day-to-day chores. "I kept a close eye on him then and helped him with advice if he had any problems," he told me.

"Other than that we led separate lives for I was a professional jockey and Richard was a young amateur hoping to make his name. To tell you the truth I barely gave him a second's thought.

"What I did notice, however, was the media attention and to this day I still cannot understand why so many newspapermen cottoned on to Richard, for as far as I was concerned he wasn't setting the world on fire at this stage in his career.

"He was a good horseman who sat nicely on his mount and he had a good pair of hands, although I always felt he rode a bit loose and didn't have tight enough control. At the same time though he knew how to present a horse to a fence and this was one characteristic which has become his trademark.

"Even so, there was nothing to suggest that his name should never be out of the racing papers and other jockeys used to come to me and ask: 'Who is this guy and what does he do?' I couldn't tell them for I didn't know!"

At that time, Richard had begun to ride out for Colin Nash who as we have seen put him up on his first winner.

He also began his association with Michael Oliver but Davies wasn't worried that Dunwoody might eventually take over from him at the Forster yard.

"As far as I was concerned I was the best," he told me. "I'm not being big-headed, but I have to be honest when I say that. The thought that Richard might become stable jockey for the Captain never entered my head."

At that time too, Davies was getting his share of

rides with David Barons and Nicky Henderson but Captain Forster, according to Hywel, would never give him enough 'space' to develop this area of activity.

"He demanded loyalty at all times and I gave it to him," he told me. –It cost me possible jobs with Barons and Henderson but I have no regrets.

"The Captain never let me down and even to this day, when I am now freelance, I still ride for him when I can and we have remained the best of friends."

Despite the blazing talent of Dunwoody which was getting a phenomenal amount of high profile reporting, Davies was still landing the odd big race winner and his happiest memory of a race against Dunwoody is not as you might imagine, that Cheltenham success on Barnbrook Again – whom he described as the best horse he had ever ridden – but in the 1989 Hennessy Gold Cup at Newbury when he rode David Elsworth's Ghofar to beat Dunwoody on Brown Windsor.

"I just nicked it," he said. "It was a fast run race on a real pro's track and Richard had gone to win it jumping the last. I was two and a half lengths down on him but managed to conjure up a late run on Ghofar and I just got up to win."

That 1990 Champion Chase also saw Davies at his best and this is the way he described it to me three years later:

"Coming off the turn Waterloo Boy and Richard were on my right and Sabin Du Loir with Scu up was on my left. I was aware that both were trying to swallow me up and all three of us were together going to the last where Scu began to lose ground. I felt the pressure from Dunwoody after the last and he headed me for a while before I got down to ride a finish I'll always be proud of."

Davies feels that Dunwoody has improved in leaps and bounds even from that race and reckons he could be champion for a long time. "He has the talent, but he is also rarely out of the headlines and that's what counts these days," he added. "I know I might sound envious but believe me I'm not for I am a close friend of Richard. I just wish he would tell me who his PR man is!"

Dunwoody's closest friend among the jockeys is fellow Irishman, Brendan Powell (he won the Aintree Grand National in 1988 on Rhyme 'N' Reason), with whom he struck up a friendship when they were both amateurs in 1983.

"I was riding for David Gandolfo at the time and Richard was with Captain Forster," Brendan said. "We both had a lot in common and I persuaded Richard to spend his summers in Ireland at my father's place, Swordlestown Stud near Naas. We used to ride out for a lot of trainers in those days including Dessie Hughes, Liam Browne and the late Peter McCreery Snr., for whom Richard finished third on Another Shot at Punchestown in 1987.

"I have always had a high regard for Richard as a horseman. To me he is total perfection – and I only wish I were as good as him," said Brendan.

"You know, when he joined the Martin Pipe stable in 1993 there were a lot of people in the game who thought that he would, to put it mildly, forget his old friends. After all, he was now champion and at the top.

"Well, believe me, this is certainly not the case. Richard is the same man he was when I first got to know him. To be frank, he's the perfect gentleman. I couldn't describe him any other way."

When Martin Pipe did not kick off the 1993-'94 season with a blaze of winners as he had done in the past, there were those who asked whether Richard had made the right move.

"But Pipe is concentrating on a better type of horse these days and you can bet that Richard will be there with the best of them. I've no doubts about that," Brendan added.

The intriguing question of Carvill's Hill then came up and I asked Brendan Powell how he felt the combination of the enigmatic chaser and the best horseman in the game would gel.

Powell had no doubts. "He'll ride Carvill's Hill just like any other horse," he said. "That's the only way to get on with him."

Carvill's Hill, of course, missed the 1992-'93 season after that infamous 1992 Cheltenham Gold Cup where he was taken on by Golden Freeze and knocked out of his stride to such an extent that he never got into the race and injured muscles in his back. After that he was retired for the immediate future.

Carvill's Hill had moved to the Pipe yard from Jim Dreaper's stables in County Dublin from where he had begun his career. Peter Scudamore rode Carvill's Hill in all his races for Pipe including the Gold Cup and his two biggest successes in the 1991-'92 season – the Welsh Grand National and the Hennessy Irish Gold Cup – after which he was made Timeform 'Chaser of the Year'.

His move from Dreaper to Pipe was greeted with a lot of scepticism in some quarters for it was felt that Pipe had nothing to teach Dreaper about the handling of the gelding who had had a history of back trouble.

And in this respect Powell would agree that Carvill's Hill jumped no better in England than he had in Ireland.

"I could see no difference," he told me. "I rode Panto Prince against him in the 'Vincent O'Brien' at Leopardstown and he never put a foot wrong for Ken Morgan even though he was beaten by Nick the Brief. I also rode Kilbannon against him in the Welsh National and he had me beaten after only three fences – and I was supposed to be on a front runner!

"Even so in that race he made mistakes and still won and he also made mistakes under Scu at Leopardstown and still won. So what was all the fuss about? In my view Ken Morgan rode him as well as any jockey and don't forget Ken was riding him when he was a novice.

"As far as Richard Dunwoody is concerned I don't see any problems. Richard is the complete professional and he'll sort out Carvill's Hill. I hope so, for I am looking forward to the big horse's return. He's a personality which the sport needs.

"In addition, with Richard Dunwoody on his back he could become one of the biggest drawing cards for many years."

CHAPTER 6

TEAMING UP WITH 'THE DUKE'

It was inevitable after West Tip's Grand National triumph that Richard Dunwoody would look to new and larger horizons – and that his services would be in even greater demand than ever before.

West Tip's success at Aintree represented his 42nd winner of the 1985-'86 National Hunt season. By the end of that same season his total would stand at 55, putting him into fifth place behind the new champion, Peter Scudamore, the man who would remain supreme until his retirement in '93 and who would be the main stumbling block to Dunwoody's own ambition to land the title of champion jump jockey in Britain.

At the beginning of the 1986-'87 season Scudamore decided to move from David 'The Duke' Nicholson's stable to Fred Winter and this meant that the No. 1 job with 'The Duke' was free. Nicholson looked no further than Dunwoody and so one of the most successful partnerships of recent times was formed.

"I was sad to see Richard go," said Captain Tim Forster. "But the fact had to be faced that he had outgrown my stable. I just hadn't the horses for him and he needed to be elsewhere. Hywel Davies was still my No. 1 and if I had been a businessman

I would have sacked him and promoted Dunwoody. That way I might have kept him. But I wouldn't do that. I had to stay loyal to Hywel.

"Richard deserved his chance and he has made the most of it. I can only remember one better jockey in my time and that was Francome. Fred Winter was a great winner finder but Francome elevated race riding to an art form and Dunwoody has achieved a similar feat. I feel at the present time he is untouchable in this respect."

So it was off to the Gloucester residence of The Duke for 1986-'87, another tilt at the jockey's title – and, of course, West Tip would be coming back for the National yet again.

Dunwoody certainly had it all to play for. He had already come to Nicholson's attention when riding as an amateur back in 1983-'84 and first rode for 'The Duke' when he finished third on Sir Girdon in a novice chase at Chepstow in 1984.

In the autumn of 1985 when he was riding No. 2 for Nicholson he had his first win for the stable on Little Sloop, a three year old mare who scored at Nottingham and was winning for the third time that term. But this was small beer.

To be a success in the racing game you need what's known as a "big horse". One who is nearly sure of winning or being placed in the major league races and thus keep the owner, trainer, or as in Dunwoody's case, jockey well entrenched in the banner headlines of the racing pages.

Although Dunwoody had now moved over to Nicholson's yard and his National triumph had established him firmly in the public eye, he was no fool. He knew that a few bad results or a year when Nicholson's horses just weren't sparking could throw him back appreciably.

So, although West Tip was still there being prepared for another National, in a sense the Michael Oliver-trained gelding had fulfilled his part in Dunwoody's career. It was very much odds against him winning the National again. Red Rums only come once in two or three generations. And most times they don't come at all.

So Dunwoody needed another partner for his expanding talents and in 1986-'87 he found just the horse in David Nicholson's Very Promising, a horse the trainer himself regards as the best Dunwoody ever rode for him.

An appropriate name for a career that was now really taking off, Very Promising was to provide Dunwoody with two of his major successes during the season – wins in the Mackeson Gold Cup at Cheltenham in November then a trip to Ireland where Dunwoody showed his talents for the first time by winning the Black and White Whisky Chase at Leopardstown's Christmas meeting.

As Dunwoody was now following in the wake of Scudamore through 'The Duke's' yard, it was only natural that he should team up with horses who had been associated with the champion in previous years. And Very Promising was undoubtedly the best of them.

Before Dunwoody sat on his back he had established a formidable record at the Cheltenham Festival meeting without actually winning. A third in Dawn Run's memorable Champion Hurdle in 1984 was followed by another third to Boreen Prince in the 1985 Arkle Trophy and then came an excellent second to Buck House in the 1986 Queen Mother Champion Chase. Nicholson must have been cursing those Irish trainers who appeared to produce good horses at just the wrong time as far as he was concerned.

Very Promising had, however, registered success in top company and in 1985-'86 had won the Walker Goddess Chase at Ascot and the Embassy Premier Chase final over the same course, something only Wayward Lad had accomplished in the same season of 1981-'82.

Dunwoody was then linked with a ready made star and he was soon to apply his exceptional talents in the style to which we had become accustomed.

The first big challenge for the partnership was the Mackeson which Half Free was trying to win for the third year in a row. Very Promising was carrying 11st 13lbs, receiving 5lbs from the penalised dual winner and the pair fought out one of the most rousing finishes of the season.

Very Promising was going well from the start and moved into the lead approaching the third last, but Dunwoody had to pull out all the stops to hold the challenge of Half Free after the final fence, getting home by two lengths.

Scudamore was the jockey on Half Free and this battle between two of the finest horsemen of our time was to be repeated on and off, season after season as both men began to dominate National Hunt racing at its highest level.

The Leopardstown win was an easier success. Very Promising, a short-priced favourite, jumped stylishly throughout, was in front from six out and drew clear relentlessly to bat the now ageing Bobsline by eight lengths.

A nice win for Dunwoody, his second in Ireland,

for he had in 1985 returned to his native Province where he won on a horse called Dearg Doom at Downpatrick. During the next summer he returned to Ulster again to ride as part of a jockeys' team at Down Royal. Hywel Davies, Peter Scudamore and Steve Smith Eccles were the other members of the team, but while Davies and Scudamore registered successes Dunwoody wasn't able to celebrate his recent National win by scoring on what could be termed his home course.

But Leopardstown made up for it. With the increased prize money in Ireland it was obvious that a race like the Black and White would draw trainers like Nicholson every year and that being the case Dunwoody would be back again to delight his growing band of Irish supporters, many of whom had heard very little about him until that National win.

With the 1987 Cheltenham Festival meeting looming, Dunwoody was set to ride Very Promising in the Queen Mother Champion Chase. But again, despite a sound effort, victory was to be denied this talented combination and it was Pearlyman who got the verdict, but only by a neck.

So for the second year running Very Promising had narrowly failed in the two milers championship, and the Gold Cup was to provide no consolation for Dunwoody, who was not on West Tip, his regular Aintree Grand National mount at that time.

Peter Hobbs, who rode Wst Tip in the Gold Cup – he started at 50/1 – was only approached by trainer Michael Oliver after the intended jockey Richard Linley had dislocated his shoulder on Gala's Image when winning the Arkle Trophy.

"Richard Dunwoody was retained to ride Charter Party and obviously he felt it had a better chance than West Tip," Peter told me. "However, before the race he came to me and said: 'Look after West Tip for me I want him for the National again.'

"Well, I did keep him out of trouble but not only that, in finishing fourth to The Thinker, after the race had been delayed by a snow-storm, I reckon West Tip ran one of his best races. Pound for pound he was up with the best of them that day, although I feel that the ground being tacky helped his chances no end. Some had said he was a good ground horse but I would have been happy to ride him with a cut in the going any time."

Hobbs rode West Tip in the Whitbread in 1989 when he was fourth again and he was also on board the gelding when he made his last National appearance in 1990 behind Mr. Frisk. "The old fellow was past it by then but he ran a good race to finish 10th," said Peter.

As for Dunwoody, his Gold Cup ended ignominiously on the sodden Cheltenham turf after Charter Party had fallen at the fifth fence. In fact, this was the second time in a row that Dunwoody had parted company with a Gold Cup mount. The previous year – the year of Dawn Run – his old Cheltenham hero Von Trappe had also fallen.

As he contemplated his prospects of winning the National again on West Tip in 1987, Richard Dunwoody would have been reasonably optimistic. Certainly the good going was against him, but against that the ten-year-old was carrying only 10lbs more than the previous year. Granted 11st 7lbs was a steadier, but did not entirely kill the chance of a horse that had run so well in the Gold

Cup. He started 5/1 favourite in a field of 40.

Surprisingly, West Tip, given what the *Chaseform Note-Book* race-reader described as "the perfect ride", was none too fluent with his jumping in the early stages and was well down the field. But he moved up among the first 10 at halfway and, after taking the inside at Bechers to save his stamina, he was a close fourth as they crossed the Melling Road for the last time. However, with Lean Ar Aghaidh setting a blistering gallop on the good ground, followed by The Tsarevitch and Maori Venture, the pace was too hot for West Tip and after being sixth at the second last he did well to survive a blunder at the last to finish fourth behind 28/1 winner Maori Venture.

"They just went too quickly for us before the second last. He did well to finish where he did. I couldn't have asked for anything more from him," said Richard, dispassionately.

No major triumph then to top off that first season with Nicholson, but a satisfying 70 winners to put himself in third place behind Peter Scudamore and Mark Dwyer.

It was the season when a man in Somerset named Martin Pipe finished sixth in the race for the trainers' title with 48 winners. Two years later his total was to rise to a staggering 208, with his No. 1 jockey, Scudamore, riding 221 against Dunwoody's third-placed 91. Who would have forecast that in 1987?

The 1986-87 season saw Dunwoody make another by now regular visit to Ireland and this time it was to the Punchestown Festival meeting in April.

More recently a major effort has been made to give a new image to this great three day meeting and make it into Ireland's own Cheltenham Festival! The effort has certainly paid off judging by the way in which top class English horses were attracted to the 1992 fixture and even more so to the 1993 renewal.

However, in 1987 when Dunwoody went for the first time, there was very little hype with the English riders having their work cut out to beat the home contingent.

Dunwoody had a fancied runner on the first day when Another Shot went for the Motor Import Handicap Chase. In an eventful finish Another Shot finished third behind Eddie Wee from the small stable of Billy Rock in County Antrim. First Noel was second a neck ahead of Another Shot but the race was turned upside down at the last fence when Fred Winter's Hazy Sunset fell just when he looked like trotting up.

So a third place for Dunwoody but he hadn't long to wait for his first Punchestown winner. High Plains was the name of the gelding who put up a highly impressive performance in the BMW Champion Novices Hurdle. Held up in the early stages while the field went a strong gallop, High Plains was smoothly brought into contention by the ice cool Dunwoody to lead approaching the second last and he sprinted clear in the straight to beat Wolf of Badanoch by eight lengths.

Dunwoody showed little emotion as he came back to the winners enclosure but he had the look of a man contented with a job well done. Once again he had shown an Irish crowd – who can be highly critical of home grown talent – the style which was making him the talk of the jumping game.

The 1987-'88 season saw Richard Dunwoody reunited again with Very Promising but this most consistent of chasers was never going to give him a Gold Cup or a National for he was very much a horse who gave his best around the two miles mark.

Very Promising had three wins that year, scoring at Devon and Exeter, Huntingdon and at Newbury where he won the Game Spirit Chase. At Devon and Newbury he beat his old rival Pearlyman, receiving 8 pounds each time, but when it came to Cheltenham and the Queen Mother Champion Chase it was the same old story, for despite the urgings of Dunwoody, Very Promising could only finish third.

It had looked for a while as though the epic battle of the previous year – when only a neck separated the two – would be repeated and approaching the last it was a toss-up. But Pearlyman soon asserted himself and Very Promising eventually lost second place to a horse called – Desert Orchid.

'Dessie' was to play a major role in Dunwoody's career at a later date but in 1988 Dunwoody had more pressing thoughts on his mind, for the day after Very Promising's defeat he was due to link up again with the horse who was – surprisingly in his view – to provide him with the headline grabbing victory to supplement West Tip's National success in 1986.

The horse was Charter Party.

CHAPTER 7

DUNWOODY GETS A 'GOLD' SURPRISE

In the countdown to the 1988 Gold Cup Richard Dunwoody was willing, on his own admission, to tell the racing world, "I think Playschool is a certainty."

As events turned out Playschool, the 100/30 favourite, was tailed off when pulled up before the third last. Richard's own mount, Charter Party, was the surprise 10/1 winner of a race marred by the putting down of the 1985 winner, the Jimmy Fitzgerald-trained Forgive 'N' Forget, who was a close third and going like a winner when shattering a hind leg approaching the third last.

Dunwoody's belief that Playschool would emerge the winner was based on solid evidence from the Form Book and little wonder the professionals backed him down to favouritism. The New Zealand-bred ten year old, trained by David Barons, had beaten Forgive 'N' Forget by eight lengths into second place in the Vincent O'Brien Irish Gold Cup Chase at Leopardstown a month previously and in his previous race at Chepstow had beaten Rhyme 'N' Reason into second place in the Coral Welsh Grand National, giving the latter 11lbs.

"The best I could have expected was to get in

the frame," Dunwoody told me. "It was a pleasant surprise to me that Charter Party should win the race, but it was a tremendous training performance by David Nicholson, for as you know Charter Party had been through the mill. He had certainly run into his share of problems.

"On the day, however, the race went remarkably smoothly and Charter Party, who had unshipped me the previous year, jumped very well. In fact, the way it evolved I had quite an easy win from Cavvies Clown and Beau Ranger."

Richard, however, would be the first to admit that the path to what was ultimately a very convincing win was made all the easier for him as a result of Cavvies Clown blundering badly at the penultimate fence and, of course, by the tragic fate that befell Forgive 'N' Forget.

In addition, a serious question remained as to why Playschool arrived at the start breathing heavily and why he ran such a lifeless race before Paul Nicholls decided that he had no other course but to pull him up.

This was the time when there was talk of a team of dopers operating in Ireland. A certain "Mister X" was mentioned after horses had run lifelessly at small meetings like Down Royal and Downpatrick in Northern Ireland. In fact, at one Downpatrick meeting the local trainer Jeremy Maxwell ordered his horse to be taken out of the parade ring because he was sure he had been "got at".

Fair enough, it's a long way from a bumper at Downpatrick to the Cheltenham Gold Cup, but there was always the suggestion of doping in connection with the Playschool affair.

Signs shown before the race matched those of

several of the Irish horses who had been "stopped" by the dopers.

Trainer David Barons said at the time that he had never been more confident about a horse or certain about his well-being. He didn't doubt that his horse had been nobbled.

And who would have thought that Charter Party would have triumphed as he did after an appalling season in 1986-'87 when he had failed to win a race? However, some shrewd judges would have noted that on February 6 at Sandown in very testing conditions he won by eight lengths from Rhyme 'N' Reason, who in his previous outing had taken the Anthony Mildmay Peter Cazalet Memorial Handicap Chase over the same course by seven lengths.

Like West Tip, Irish-bred Charter Party had gone through the sales ring three times before beginning his career under David Nicholson, who had bought him at Doncaster Spring Sales for 8,000 guineas as a four-year-old.

His pedigree wasn't startling for his sire Document hadn't got a winner of note, but Nicholson said he wasn't worried by the horse's family tree. He bought him because of his looks.

Charter Party's career went smoothly at first and he had three good seasons over fences, the climax being two top races at Cheltenham – the Ritz Club at the Festival in 1986 when ridden by Peter Scudamore, he beat Catch Phrase three lengths, and the Golden Miller Chase at the Cheltenham April meeting.

But according to Nicholson he had been "gurgling" after these races and the decision was taken in the summer of 1986 to have the gelding undergo hobday and soft palate operations in order to help his wind.

His breathing improved immensely but he failed to enter the winners enclosure once during the 1986-'87 season and he fell in the 1987 Gold Cup.

The next affliction to hit him was intermittent lameness during the 1987-'88 season. He ran only four times in all during that season and when he lined up for the Gainsborough Chase at Sandown in February, 1988 he hadn't won a race for 21 months. A Gold Cup winner the following month? You could have had any price!

Charter Party jumped soundly throughout and, as we have seen, was too good for Rhyme 'N' Reason and also had Desert Orchid behind him in third place.

Granted, Charter Party received 17lbs from Desert Orchid that day, but it was still a very encouraging performance from the "cripple", who, as luck would have it, was lame once more after this race.

"We knew something was hurting him but could not find out what it was," Nicholson said later. "It showed when he was cantering or walking but once he warmed up it disappeared. We didn't know what it was and feared to X-ray his feet in case he would have to be retired."

Charter Party, however, was still an enthusiastic eater and appeared also to love racing. In home gallops shortly before the Gold Cup he beat Very Promising and another of Dunwoody's highly successful partners, Long Engagement, over a mile and a quarter. Not bad, but the doubts must still have been lingering in the minds of Nicholson and Dunwoody.

Desert Orchid didn't take Charter Party on in the Gold Cup, but went instead for the Two Miles Chase. Cavvies Clown from the same David Elsworth stable did, however, line up with the rest of them, including the tough battler Rhyme 'N' Reason.

Beau Ranger and Golden Friend made the early running until Cavvies Clown took it up for the final time with Run and Skip, Charter Party, Forgive 'N' Forget and Beau Ranger in close attendance.

Then came the fateful fourth from home where Forgive 'N' Forget met total disaster and Rhyme 'N' Reason also exited.

Even then the drama wasn't over. The race was now between Cavvies Clown and Charter Party, but at the second last Cavvies Clown made that massive blunder sending Simon Sherwood skywards – only for him to land back in the saddle! Despite the magnificence of the recovery, however, this accident handed the race to Dunwoody and Charter Party on a plate.

Charter Party's feet were eventually X-rayed and it was discovered that he had navicular disease caused by thrombosis of his front feet.

Happily he was able to race again the following season when he was kept in a stable with a rubber cover on the floor. Pads were also fitted to his shoes.

He went for a repeat win in the 1989 Gold Cup but by this time there was a new hero galloping over the horizon. After a number of hiccups Desert Orchid at last showed himself to be a Cheltenham horse by justifying 5/2 favouritism in winning a memorable Gold Cup with Simon Sherwood in the saddle.

Charter Party by then an eleven year old ran an excellent race in taking third place, but it went entirely unnoticed by the crowd who were in a frenzy of excitement as they watched their hero Desert Orchid just get up to beat Yahoo and Tom Morgan by one-and-a-half lengths.

Two months on, Dunwoody would get the call to ride Britain's favourite racehorse. But no one was thinking that far ahead as Simon Sherwood rode proudly into the winner's enclosure on that March day in 1989.

Dunwoody's total of winners had also moved up to 79 in the Jockeys Championship which took him into third place behind Scudamore on 132 and Chris Grant on 80. That coveted title still seemed a long way off. And, of course, the following year – when Pipe and Scudamore smashed every record in sight – Dunwoody must have felt that the cherished goal was further away than ever.

The 1987-'88 season – the year of Dunwoody's Gold Cup triumph, on Charter Party, also saw the Ulsterman join the "marriage stakes".

Two very special equine guests attended Richard's wedding to Carol Abraham – West Tip, his National hero and of course, Charter Party. They were brought along specially to the reception which was held in a huge marquee surrounded by acres of rolling Oxfordshire countryside.

"It was the sort of reception I had always imagined," Carol told me. "The marquee we had hired was much too large for my own home so we contacted some friends of ours, Gordon and Jill Pill and they agreed to let us have their spread. West Tip and Charter Party had to come along as well of course and they were stabled at Michael Robinson's yard, for I was working for him at the time.

"West Tip, would you believe, was even brought into the marquee and he behaved impeccably, but Charter Party was a different story. He appeared not to like my white wedding dress and shied away from it. Still, nothing was broken and the guests didn't have any garments chewed, so I suppose that was a bonus," she laughed.

Among the 300 guests were many of Richard's owners and of course trainer David Nicholson, but also on the guest list were two of Richard's relatives from Northern Ireland who were better known in a non-racing world.

Terry Hill, one of Belfast's best known auto dealers, won fame in the world of motor cycle sport and was in his youth one of Ireland's leading riders in endurance trials including the Scottish Six Days event, the Olympics of the sport in Britain. His wife Betty however had genuine racing connections for she is George Dunwoody's cousin.

"My mother was a Graham from Monaghan, and my brother Herbie Eakin was a close friend of George's in the early days when they were both wild about horses," Betty Hill told me.

"We were delighted to have received the invitation to Richard's wedding and I can tell you it was a truly memorable occasion, especially with West Tip and Charter Party stealing all the attention."

Jimmy Burgess was also invited but unfortunately couldn't travel. However, jockey Brendan Powell and his parents made it and gave the occasion a suitable Irish flavour.

For Carol it was naturally a day to savour and

one she might have been dreaming of the first day she set eyes on Richard. "That was when he arrived at Captain Forster's yard," she told me. "I was only 15 at the time and I was stabling my ponies near the Captain's place. I liked the look of Richard and he did take me out once when I was 16 but really there were older girls there to take his fancy.

"It wasn't until Christmas 1985 that we really got together. You know my grandfather was a blacksmith for Captain Forster and also owned the village pub so we used to gather there to socialise.

"Richard could sometimes be found there with his pals and we gradually got to know each other better. By this time I had left school and was working for David Gandolfo. Then when I joined Henrietta Knight at Lockinge I came into close contact with Richard for he used to come over to take out Henrietta's point to pointers. I suppose from early 1986, the year he won the National, you could say we were what the Americans call an item."

Since her marriage Carol Dunwoody has developed her own career and rides out regularly for Henry Candy. Here again there is an Ulster connection for Candy trains for the famous Barnett family from Donaghadee. One of the best known Barnett colts was Master Willie, second in the Derby and winner of the Benson and Hedges Gold Cup at York. Time Charter and Nicholas Bill are other Barnett horses to have been trained at the Candy stable.

Apart from riding out, Carol also has a career as an amateur jockey and this keeps her occupied during Richard's long and hungry search for winners at places like Hexham, Perth and Sedgefield.

"Of course, I miss him when he's away," she told me, "but when he does get time off we do our best to spend it together."

CHAPTER 8

DUNWOODY FINDS A CHAMPION IN KRIBENSIS

Richard Dunwoody knew the first day he rode Kribensis that Sheikh Mohammed's gelding was something special – "a smashing horse," as he put it. He regards himself as having been privileged to have been associated with the grey "and lucky to fall in for the ride in the first place."

Kribensis was to provide Richard not alone with a scintillating Daily Express Triumph Hurdle win in 1988 but with his first Champion Hurdle success in 1990, to add to the Grand National win in 1986 on West Tip and the Gold Cup victory on Charter Party in 1988.

In a way by winning the Champion Hurdle *after* the Grand National and Gold Cup successes Richard Dunwoody was doing things somewhat in reverse when one recalled how famous riders of earlier decades hit the jackpot in the Aintree Grand National after first landing the Champion Hurdle or Gold Cup or both.

Martin Molony's brother, Tim, for example, had won two of his four successive Champion Hurdles (Hatton's Grace, 1951 and Sir Ken, 1952-'53) before he won the Gold Cup in 1953 on Knock Hard, though he missed out on a National triumph. Fred Winter had won two Champion Hurdles (Clair

Soleil, 1955 and Fare Time, 1959) before he landed his first Gold Cup on Saffron Tartan in 1961, the year he would win another 'Champion' on Eborneezer. In 1962 he won the Gold Cup again on Mandarin and took his second Grand National on Kilmore, having won it for the first time in 1957 on Sundew.

Tommy Carberry had recorded two successive Gold Cup triumphs on L'Escargot (1970 and '71) before winning the Grand National on Raymond Guest's horse in 1975 while Peter Scudamore who won his second Champion Hurdle on Granville Again in 1993, – his first was Celtic Shot – did not enjoy the honour before his retirement the same year, of riding either a Gold Cup winner or a Grand National winner. And John Francome, rated by many as one of the finest of all National Hunt jockeys of modern times, while he won the Champion Hurdle on Sea Pigeon (1981) and the Gold Cup on Midnight Court (1978), missed out on a National success.

Therefore, in winning the three most prestigious races on the National Hunt calendar before he was crowned champion jockey in Britain for the first time, Richard Dunwoody could be thankful that the Hinge of Destiny had been with him right from the start of his career when as an 'unknown' amateur he burst on the scene with those four winners in the one afternoon at Hereford.

Now the Hinge of Fate worked again for him in the manner in which he came in for the ride on Kribensis in the Triumph Hurdle in 1988.

Steve Smith-Eccles was booked by Nicky Henderson to ride the strongly-fancied Surf Board in the 'Triumph' and that meant that Michael

Stoute, trainer of Kribensis, had to look for a deputy. Naturally he chose Dunwoody.

"Michael rang me one day and asked me to ride Kribensis in his next outing at Huntingdon," Dunwoody recalled. "I was delighted, of course. He won the Chatteris Fen Hurdle beating Young Snugfit by five lengths. It was the sort of performance that gave me high hopes that he would win the Triumph."

Kribensis was the only jumper in Michael Stoute's Newmarket stable. Stoute had finished runner-up in the 1987 Flat racing trainers list and, frankly, until Kribensis hit the headlines as a class hurdler, he was more associated in the mind of the racing public with summer days at Epsom, Ascot, Goodwood or the Curragh challenging for Classic events or other major races.

When asked why he trained only one horse 'over the sticks', the urbane Stoute shrugged his shoulders and replied, with a mischievous gleam in his eye: "No one else has asked me to train for them!"

After proving himself a useful middle-distance winner on the Flat, Kribensis was obviously better than the average recruit to hurdling and his debut over timber was eagerly looked forward to at the Doncaster meeting on January 30, 1988.

The race was the Brewer's Hurdle (4-Y-O) and Kribensis, ridden by Steve Smith-Eccles started the even-money favourite in a field of sixteen. His jumping was rather deliberate, particularly at the outset, and he had to battle to shake off Brendan Powell and 7/1 shot Eskimo Mite, which he beat by a neck. However, as *Chaseform Note-Book* noted it was "a quiet educational run" and Kribensis had won cleverly without in any way being pushed to the limit. Naturally, he was immediately installed favourite for the Triumph Hurdle.

It was a different Kribensis who justified the odds of 8/11 laid on him at Huntingdon on February 23 – the day Richard Dunwoody first rode him – and so fluent and authoritative was his success that Surf Board was now seen as the only real obstacle to his taking the big Cheltenham prize.

Ironically, Surf Board which was to start 4/1 joint favourite with Kribensis, after leading from half-way to the second last, faded right out of it and the form seemed too bad to be true. However, Flat form experts noted that Kribensis had conceded two stone to him at Royal Ascot in June of the previous year and had still beaten him.

The pace was slower than usual for the Triumph Hurdle but Dunwoody had Kribensis up among the leaders from early on.

Kribensis wasn't extending himself, hurdling fluently, and when the leading contenders quickened down the hill Dunwoody was able to sit against Kribensis until it became necessary to watch Chatam and Peter Scudamore after the second last.

Kribensis soon demolished not only Chatam but Surf Board, South Parade, Wingspan and Chesham Squire, making it very obvious as he beat the 66/1 shot Wahiba by an easy three lengths that he was a very good juvenile who would be top rated for the following year's Champion Hurdle, much as had been the case with Persian War 20 year earlier.

Dunwoody certainly thought so. "He was a smashing horse to ride and one who might have run up a sequence of big race wins at Cheltenham had he kept sound," he told me. "But that's the way it goes."

But quick-actioned Kribensis was a horse who was seen at his best on a sound – if not fast – surface. Heavy rain had softened the going considerably when the field lined up for the 1989 Champion Hurdle, for which Richard Dunwoody's mount started a warm 11/8 favourite, though it was only his seventh race over hurdles.

It was hard to oppose him on form, as he had been very impressive in beating Floyd by two lengths in the Top Rank Christmas Hurdle at Kempton in December and won his two previous outings by twelve lengths and five lengths respectively. So he was coming to the Festival meeting with an unblemished record for the season.

Those who had backed Kribensis as if he was a certainty, felt it was only a case of collecting when he took up the running at the home turn. But once he was taken on, he found nothing in the testing going and was soon headed, the 50/1 shot Beech Road and Richard Guest coming home two lengths ahead of 6/1 shot Celtic Chief with Celtic Shot and Peter Scudamore third. Kribensis had to be content with seventh place in a field of fifteen.

Still, Richard Dunwoody did not lose faith in the grey and knew that on good ground he would prove the 1989 Champion form all wrong.

And this was to be proved with a vengeance the following year.

Again Kribensis arrived at the Festival meeting with an unbeaten record for the season in his three preliminary runs justifying 4/7 favouritism on his seasonal debut at Newcastle in November '89, then repeating his victory of 1988 in the Top Rank Christmas Hurdle at Kempton, when starting 4/6 favourite, and taking the Kingswell Hurdle at Wincanton in February '90 by four lengths from Island Set. Those who took the risk of backing him ante-post realised that everything depended on the going on the opening day at Cheltenham '90.

The going was fast but Beech Road, the '89 winner started 2/1 favourite with Kribensis at 95/40 second favourite.

Champion Hurdle Day '90 was likened by the cynics to Derby Day in the sense that the first two horses home were owned by Sheikh Mohammed and Robert Sangster. Sangster owned Nomadic Way, who tracked his stable-companion Sudden Victory to the fourth last and Peter Scudamore had him in the lead at the penultimate flight. But Dunwoody timed his run to perfection on Kribensis and pouncing at the last, stormed up the hill to clip the course record by a second as he finished three lengths ahead of Nomadic Way with the 150/1 shot Past Glories third.

Kribensis thus became the first grey to win the race in 52 years.

It was a high point for Dunwoody who told me: "That was my third Cheltenham ride on Kribensis and I had never had an easier win. He was always going well and at the time I felt he was sure to emulate See You Then and win the race three years running. He might have done so but for the fact that he later ran into problems and had to be taken out of training. It was a great pity for all concerned."

In fact, the grey missed a year through breaking blood vessels and had reportedly chipped a bone in his near hind leg in December, 1991.

In the 1992 Champion Hurdle, according to Dunwoody, Kribensis badly injured his off hind leg when he hit the upright of the third hurdle and after that he was eased and finished 14th behind the ill-fated Royal Gait.

Sheikh Mohammed watched the 1990 Champion Hurdle live via satellite from Dubai and afterwards his racing manager, Ulsterman Anthony Stroud, said: "The Sheikh would have loved to have been here but matters of State kept him at home."

On that Tuesday evening, the prophets of doom were predicting that Arab oil money would dominate National Hunt racing and that the best material would be snapped up by the Sheikhs – and that the Willie Lomans of our time could forget about providing us with those kind of romantic stories that we had always seen as an integral part of the jumping game.

But in a corner of Wales a farmer-cum owner-cum small trainer was not thinking of Sheikh Mohammed dreaming dreams watching Kribensis via satellite television in Dubai winning the Champion Hurdle; he was concentrating his mind totally on his cows and on a chaser called Norton's Coin winning the Tote Gold Cup.

The area of Wales we are talking about is around Carmarthen in the west of the Principality and they were more accustomed to setting the bonfires alight for rugby heroes than for racing horses. On the evening of March 15, 1990 in the village of Nantgaredig, not far from Carmarthen which had given the legendary stand-off half, Barry John and the flying winger, Gerald Davies to Welsh rugby they put up a banner which read: "Welcome Home

Norton's Coin."

Sirrell Griffiths milked 70 Friesian cows at 5.30a.m. on that never-to-be-forgotten Thursday morning before driving his cattle truck (he did not have a horse-box) to Cheltenham to take on Desert Orchid, the pride of England, with Richard Dunwoody in the saddle.

The thousands and thousands of admirers of "Dessie" – the many who would not even contemplate the defeat of the reigning champion chaser – allowed Norton's Coin to go off at 100/1 while Desert Orchid started 10/11 favourite.

It was a fairytale story in itself how Norton's Coin beat Toby Tobias by three-parts-of-a-length with the now eleven-years-old Desert Orchid four lengths further away third, after Dunwoody had him placed perfectly to win at the penultimate fence – but his measure was taken at the last, though as always he ran his heart out. Sirrell Griffiths had disproved the theory that you need to have the limitless resources of the Arab Sheikhs to win one of the major prizes at the Festival meeting.

We could sleep contentedly again in our beds . . . Cheltenham would continue to throw up the kind of romantic stories that had Sirrell Griffiths telling Geoff Lester of the *Sporting Life:* "When I got back home to the village from Cheltenham we were met by TV crews and hundreds of well-wishers from near and far and I had to send one of the boys out for ten bottles of Scotch. There wasn't much left by the time they all went – I can promise you."

Kribensis wasn't the only Sheikh Mohammed hurdler Dunwoody became acquainted with. Highland Bud, trained by David Nicholson, was his mount in the 1989 Daily Express Triumph

Hurdle and he had every reason to believe that this one would follow up the success of Kribensis in the same event the previous year.

Highland Bud had won the Ulster Harp Derby at Down Royal in 1988 when trained by John Oxx and had also finished third in the Ulster St. Leger over the same course. I remember this tough little battler winning at Down Royal as I was part of the BBC broadcasting team which beamed the Down Royal meeting to Britain on a nationwide basis. Therefore, I was more than a casual observer when I found out that Richard Dunwoody had linked up with 'Bud' and followed the horse's progress intently on the way to the Festival meeting.

Highland Bud, in fact, was bidding to complete a three-timer in the Triumph Hurdle as he had justified 15/8 favouritism when winning by ten lengths at Newbury in December and Richard Dunwoody followed this up by taking the Food Brokers 'Finesse' Hurdle at Cheltenham on January 28 in easy fashion from two previous winners in 8/11 favourite, Enemy Action, the mount of Peter Scudamore, and Propero.

The going was officially 'yielding' that day at Cheltenham but it was heavy on the day of the Triumph Hurdle and, as in the case of Kribensis, it was to prove Highland Bud's undoing as he lost his unbeaten record over hurdles.

Starting at 8/1, Richard Dunwoody always had him beautifully placed and he looked a winner when he beat off the challenges of Don Valentino and Royal Derbi but in the testing ground the stamina of the 66/1 outsider Ikdam caught him out and he was beaten by one-and-a-half lengths having given a most courageous display in conditions that were all against him.

Highland Bud later finished five lengths second to Vayrua in the Glenlivet Anniversary Hurdle at Liverpool but ran below his best when third to Royal Derbi in the Guinness Trophy Champion EBF Hurdle at the Punchestown Festival meeting.

Shortly after this, he was sold at the Doncaster Spring Sales and broke the record of £105,000 guineas following which which he was shipped to America to be trained by Jonathan Sheppard. This opened up a new vista for Richard Dunwoody. He retained his link with Highland Bud and won the 1989 Breeders Cup Chase in October, followed by the Colonial Cup. These successes saw Highland Bud take the Eclipse Award for the champion chaser in the United States.

Most remarkable of all, Highland Bud broke down after the 1989 Colonial Cup. He was nursed back and contested the 1992 Breeders Cup Chase at New York's Belmont Park where, with Richard Dunwoody up, he scored again – a singular triumph considering the serious setback he had suffered the previous year. "A tough little horse," said Richard in tribute to the chaser that had brought him headlines in the American Racing Press. "You don't get many like that in chasing these days."

In the 1989 Grand National Richard Dunwoody came within seven lengths of recording a second triumph in the big Aintree race on gallant West Tip, now a twelve year old.

West Tip had now become as familiar to the public as Red Rum was in his prime and with a win and two fourths to his credit, he had become an Aintree "specialist", who could be guaranteed to give a good account of himself, no matter what

102

the conditions.

In 1988 carrying the steadier of 11-7, West Tip was one of five horses with every chance three out, one of them being Monanore, trained at Templemore, County Tipperary by Bill Harney and ridden this time by Tom Taaffe, son of the legendary Pat. The previous day's heavy rain and the weight saw West Tip unable to get in a meaningful challenge and Dunwoody had to be content with fourth place behind Monanore as Rhyme 'N' Reason – like Dunwoody, bred in Ulster – scored a remarkable triumph in the hands of Irish-born jockey, Brendan Powell from Durham Edition. The winner almost came to a standstill at Bechers first time round when landing on his head and sliding along the ground – but Powell brilliantly gave him time to make this one of the great recoveries in the recent history of the National.

West Tip, carrying 10-11 in 1989, started at 12/1 with the 1987 Gold Cup winner, The Thinker at 10/1 and Durham Edition at 15/2 and Dixton House, the favourite at 7/1.

There is little doubt that West Tip ran his best race since his National triumph three years earlier.

For once Dunwoody decided on a change of tactics and kept West Tip up front disputing the lead for most of the first circuit. Approaching the second last, however, West Tip appeared to be finding the pace too much for him, but, amazingly, he rallied and went on again to finish a seven lengths second to another National veteran, 28/1 shot Little Polveir, another Northern Ireland-bred horse, from Ballygowan, not far from Dunwoody's childhood home.

As usual West Tip jumped soundly and

Dunwoody reported "he was foot perfect and gave me a fantastic ride, as good a ride, in fact, as when he won the race." There could be no higher praise.

The Thinker finished third in a National which was a watershed in the history of the race, for this was the day when ill-fated Brown Trix found himself in the brook at Bechers and couldn't get out – in full view of the TV cameras.

Brown Trix and Seeandem were both killed at this fence and in May of that same year, the alterations to the course were introduced which have since been a source of keen debate among aficionados of National Hunt racing.

Is the National course now too easy? In 1990 Mr Frisk smashed the race record when appearing to brush through the once fearsome obstacles and Dunwoody added his own views when he told me: "The National should remain a tough test for horse and rider. That's its appeal. It's a unique occasion and I wouldn't like to see it becoming any easier than it has since the fences were altered in 1990.

"In the years since I won it on West Tip I have noticed a change. The fences are definitely easier which means horses can brush through them and lower their jumping.

"I feel this is bad for the horses as it instils a lack of respect for the obstacles. As a result, horses tend to jump lower and lower and end up on the floor. That's what happened to Rinus when he fell in 1991.

"If horses feel that the fences are stiff and have to be jumped then they will jump them cleanly and the race will certainly be safer. I am also against any reduction in the field.

"Some people who are totally ignorant of race

riding feel that 40 is too high a number of horses. This is rubbish for Aintree is the widest course in the country. There's a load of room for horses to run unlike other courses where there is very little daylight."

CHAPTER 9

DUNWOODY AND THE DESSIE DAYS

In May of 1989 Richard Dunwoody took a fateful call from Richard Burridge, owner of Desert Orchid.

"He asked me if I was interested in riding the horse," recalled Dunwoody. "I replied 'yes, of course' – but pointed out that I would have to clear it not alone with David Nicholson but with Nicky Henderson, who by now had second claim on me. They told me to go ahead, so Dessie and I linked up.

"To be honest, I felt not only a little bit nervous at taking over the nation's hero, but privileged to have been asked at all."

The partnership would see Dunwoody win the King George VI Rank Chase two years running (1989 and '90) on the dashing grey and also the Jameson Irish Grand National (1990), though Dessie would fail in his bid to make it two Gold Cups back-to-back in 1990, going down in the famous Norton's Coin upset referred to earlier.

Desert Orchid had won the 1988 'King George' with Simon Sherwood in the saddle by four lengths, having already taken it in 1986. Richard Dunwoody was setting out to make it a three-timer when the field of six lined up for the 1989 renewal.

He sweated up in the preliminaries and his jumping on this occasion was mostly brilliant – but at the same time he gave his legion of admirers, including those present at Kempton that day and the many more looking in on television, spasms of alarm when he put in a clumsy one at the open ditch (12th) and again wasn't foot-perfect at the next. However, once he regained his composure he left his rivals trailing as he took the last three fences in style to win going away by eight lengths form Barnbrook Again and Yahoo a further seven lengths behind third.

Those not stirred by the wave of emotion that always surrounded any of the grey's major triumphs would have concluded that Desert Orchid, who would be eleven by the time of Cheltenham '90, was now a little bit past his peak, though the glory days were not entirely dimmed. Remember he had been on the go from the 1982/'83 season. The zest for racing reappeared from time to time and there was still the odd smashing performance to follow. But at the same time there was an inconsistency about Desert Orchid's efforts that was disturbing to those who in the totality of their admiration had come to the point where they thought there was no chink at all in his armour and would even have backed him to beat Arkle, had he been a contemporary.

For example, the first time Richard Dunwoody rode Desert Orchid – at Wincanton on November 9, 1989 – he had cantered over his sole opponent, Roll-A-Joint to win by twelve lengths. Next time out at Sandown, however, he went down to Long Engagement in the Tingle Creek Chase. Granted the distance (2m) was short of his best and he was conceding two stone to the winner but the doubters, while ignoring the pulsating manner he literally flew his fences in a classic exhibition of jumping, were still given enough ammunition to pose the pertinent question: 'Is Dessie on the decline?'

Trainer David Elsworth countered by stating emphatically that this was not the case, that Desert Orchid was short of a race and that his main objective initially that season was again the King George on the way to another crack at the Gold Cup.

According to Elsworth, they really got "stuck into him" as they prepared for the big Kempton event– and it certainly paid off.

However, the eight lengths that Desert Orchid put between him and Barnbrook Again had to be viewed in proper perspective. Barnbrook Again was not a true three-mile chaser when it came to a race like the King George. True he won over the distance at Newbury on February 10, 1990 on his way to the Festival meeting but his task was made much easier that day when Toby Tobias, the 8/11 favourite, made a hash of the tenth and lost his rider in the process. That two miles was his best distance was proved beyond any shadow of doubt when he mastered Waterloo Boy and Dunwoody in the 1990 Queen Mother Champion Chase at Cheltenham.

When, the following day, Desert Orchid only managed third place in the Gold Cup behind Norton's Coin and Toby Tobias, Dunwoody was making no excuses. "He was beaten fairly and squarely," said Richard.

"Ten of Spades did take me on from the front

going out on the second circuit and he pushed me out a bit turning into the straight, but this could not be used as an excuse for a defeat by four-and-three-quarter lengths. The very fast ground must have contributed to Desert Orchid's performance, although he had won his Whitbread on a similar surface two years earlier."

It can be argued that Desert Orchid might not even have won in 1989 had the ill-fated Ten Plus not fallen at the third last, having jumped into the lead.

"Losing Ten Plus in that Gold Cup was dreadful, you know," the late Fulke Walwyn said in the course of an interview with Christopher Poole of the *Evening Standard* in the 1990-'91 edition of the *Irish Racing Annual*. "He would have won in my view. Kevin Mooney thought he had Desert Orchid cold when Ten Plus fell and I agree with him."

When Dunwoody returned to the unsaddling enclosure after Norton's Coin had silenced the thousands who had come to cheer Dessie to victory, there wasn't the frosty welcome waiting him that might easily have been expected, considering that the people's champion was the first odds-on favourite (10/11) in sixteen years.

"Of course David Elsworth and Richard Burridge were disappointed but they accepted that the horse had run a smashing race," said Richard. "You can't win them all in racing. I detected no sense of recrimination."

Elsworth showed the unique spirit of National Hunt racing by dashing over to shake the hand of Sirrell Griffiths, who was surrounded by well-wishers – and still looking for his cap after jockey Graham McCourt had whisked it off his head in jubilation when he came in on the winner.

There was consolation for Dunwoody for his defeat in the Gold Cup when Desert Orchid won the Jameson Irish Grand National on Easter Monday, April 16, '90 and in the process was accorded a tremendous reception by the thousands who thronged the Fairyhouse venue. Indeed, Dunwoody noted that the reception was as good as anything he had experienced when winning on Dessie on an English racecourse.

Desert Orchid was among the better class horses to travel for the event. Run right-handed and with the weights limited to a two stone range, everything was tipped in his favour. It was not surprising that Burridge and Elsworth plumped for the Irish National rather than the Whitbread Gold Cup.

Dessie made much of the running and had the prize practically in his grasp when he made a dreadful error at the final fence.

Many a good horse would have fallen and a less-cool and less-alert jockey might have come off but Dunwoody was magnificent in that moment of crisis in maintaining his partnership with the grey. Having cleared the ultimate fence, Desert Orchid galloped on to win by twelve lengths from Barney Burnett with Have a Barney third.

"He was so far clear he only had to stay on his feet but at the same time he was very tired and I was conscious of this," Richard said. "He just clipped the top of the fence and I sat tight. Thankfully, he stayed on his feet."

Would Desert Orchid have won the Aintree Grand National? As absorbing a question for debates by winter fires as asking: Would Arkle have treated the Aintree fences with the same disdain as he treated the fences on every other racecourse, including Cheltenham and Fairyhouse?

Pat Taaffe had no doubt whatsoever that Arkle with his uncanny jumping ability would have adapted to Aintree and added the National to his three authoritative Cheltenham Gold Cup triumphs but Anne Duchess of Westminster would not allow her beloved chaser to contest the race because she feared he might be badly injured and would then have to be put down. She could not contemplate that thought.

After Desert Orchid had won the King George for the third time, the news broke that he was to be entered for the 1990 Aintree National. It immediately had the effect of setting public opinion alight.

Normally staid people got passionately involved in the 'should he?' or should he not?' debate which developed an intensity never known before in racing on this side of the Atlantic.

The tabloids had a field day, of course, and even held polls among their readers. The vote against risking Desert Orchid at Aintree was overwhelmingly against (in the *Daily Mail* poll, for example, less than 50 readers were in favour of allowing the grey to take his chance, while 9,000 voted solidly against it).

Desert Orchid was given 12-2 in the original handicap. It was obvious that the handicapper had gone out of his way to be fair and was as anxious as every aficionado of the jumping game to see how the horse would fare in the race. David Elsworth was very anxious to run Dessie and his viewpoint on the subject was summed up thus: "If it's not fair for a superb jumper like Desert Orchid to run in the National, it's not fair for any horse to contest the race . . ."

But the little old dears, who sit in armchairs and make their judgements from what they see of horses falling at those 'terrible' fences at Aintree, had made up their minds and no argument was going to sway them. Professionals who should have known far better came in behind them. The lobby against Desert Orchid running became so powerful that even if the Burridges had wanted to run him, they would have found it extremely difficult to swim against the tide of public opinion.

A survey carried out by Ladbrokes had revealed that, not alone was Desert Orchid Britain's favourite racehorse, but he was more widely recognised than a number of public figures, including the Chancellor of the Exchequer, Norman Lamont. Those campaigning against the export of live horses for slaughter actually pressed Dessie into service to make an appearance outside No. 10 Downing Street. How's that for celebrity status?

But if one had been able to cut through all the hype and have managed to get a proper debate going on the subject, involving personalities who had been born into the National Hunt game and lived for the sport, then it would have been shown that Lanzarote and Forgive 'N' Forget, the 1985 Gold Cup winner, were killed in action at Cheltenham and also, as we have seen already, Ten Plus in the 1989 Gold Cup. Where, one might ask, was the outcry from the little old ladies and others when Ten Plus was put down – how many of them demanded beforehand that Desert Orchid should not be risked in this 'dangerous' race?

The brilliant Golden Cygnet, destined to be a

winner of the Champion Hurdle, had suffered injuries from which he would not survive in a hurdle race at Ayr. Then, Dawn Run, following a Gold Cup triumph in 1986 in the hands of Jonjo O'Neill which had been acclaimed in a manner not seen at Cheltenham since Arkle beat Mill House in the 1964 Gold Cup, died in action that same summer in France.

True, those against running Desert Orchid in the National could point to Alverton being killed at Bechers in 1989 but, against that, Garrison Savannah, the 1991 Gold Cup winner, went on to contest the Aintree Grand National the same year and came very close to beating the winner, Seagram.

And The Thinker, the 1987 Gold Cup winner, was third in the 1989 Grand National behind Little Polveir and West Tip.

"The National is a marvellous race, a great spectacle and an easier race to win nowadays than the Whitbread Gold Cup," said David Elsworth. "I thought it would be a great race for Desert Orchid to win."

"But I respect the views of the owners and I can see their point," he added.

Desert Orchid was taken out at the forfeit stage in February, 1990.

What did Dunwoody, the National specialist, think about all the controversy. "I can only speculate, but I believe that Desert Orchid might just have won the National. His jumping should not have been a problem since the fences are so much easier and he would certainly have got the trip."

The diplomat in Dunwoody did not permit him to say anymore.

Desert Orchid won a record-breaking fourth King George in December '90 (up to then he had been on three wins with Wayward Lad) and returned to a reception that outstripped anything he had known in a career that would extend over nine seasons.

He came home twelve lengths in front of Toby Tobias with the French challenger, The Fellow – then only five – a further five lengths behind in third place.

Richard Dunwoody's link with Desert Orchid was making his name known to thousands who might otherwise never have become acquainted with his ranking and achievements as a National Hunt jockey. Channel 4 reported that it had a viewing public of 2.9 million for the King George – its second biggest of the year for racing (the Derby was No. 1).

Desert Orchid, now 12, again failed in the Gold Cup, finishing third behind the 16/1 shot, the Jenny Pitman-trained Garrison Savannah, who beat The Fellow by a short head in a tremendous battle from the last fence.

The details of these and other races contested by Desert Orchid have been fully chronicled in Jonathan Powell's admirable book, *Desert Orchid: The Story of a Champion* and in the authoritative *The Desert Orchid Years*, produced by *Timeform*, with a Foreword by David Elsworth.

Suffice it to say that the *Timeform* writers hit the nail on the head when they argued that the celebrations of some of Desert Orchid's performances were excessive, especially after his brave win in extremely testing conditions in the 1989 Gold Cup. "To mention Desert Orchid in the same breath as

Arkle, as some did, is something no experienced and rational critic of the game can stomach." *Timeform* concluded: "Desert Orchid will leave a memory of brilliant jumping and grinding courage but as things stand you don't have to go back to the halcyon days of Arkle and his brilliant contemporaries, Flyingbolt and Mill House to find chasers of at least equal merit. The Gold Cup winners, Burrough Hill Lad and Captain Christy, for example, attained ratings of 184 and 182 respectively."

Desert Orchid's highest *Timeform* rating was 187 and this was bettered by only three jumpers those stars of the Sixties, Arkle, Flyingbolt and Mill House.

Arkle, the incomparable, achieved a rating of 212. And *Timeform* in his final season described him as 'the greatest chaser ever'. Mill House was rated at 191.

Desert Orchid won thirty-four races from forty-seven starts but his record could in no way compare with Arkle who, according to *Timeform*, "at the height of his powers looked as close to unbeatable as any horse is ever likely to be."

Arkle was beaten only four times in 26 chases, including his final appearance when he broke down contesting the King George VI Chase in 1966. He was in his prime then as a nine-year-old and arguably he could, if he had stayed sound, gone on to equal – if not surpass – Golden Miller's record of five Gold Cup victories.

Arkle carried 12-7 each time he won the Hennessy Gold Cup and the same weight when he won the Whitbread Gold Cup, the Gallaher Gold Cup and the SGB Handicap Chase.

But in the final analysis it was his three successive Gold Cup triumphs (1964-'66) and the beating of Mill House in the first two that put him head and shoulders above Desert Orchid, who had Yahoo and Charter Party, the 1988 winner, behind him when taking his one Gold Cup in 1989. Yahoo and Charter Party do not figure in any debates on the great chasers of modern times. And could you imagine Arkle being beaten in the Gold Cup by a 100/1 outsider like Norton's Coin, as Desert orchid was in 1990?

No, if Cheltenham is the racecourse where the real champions inevitably show greatness against opposition that really counts, then Arkle left no doubt whatsoever about where he stands in National Hunt racing history by the sheer merit of his three-timer in the Gold Cup. He was so much head and shoulders above all the rest that, outside of Mill House – the only one capable of living with him at levels – only two others were in the field for the 1964 Gold Cup.

It was the same story in 1965. In 1966 the field for the Blue Riband of chasing was five. In the 'Year of Desert Orchid', thirteen contested the Gold Cup (a few in the field who thought they had a hope but were no-hopers really!).

In truth Desert Orchid, while he could turn on breath-taking performances on a 'Park course' like Kempton, was overall a disappointment when it came to Cheltenham. The ultimate judgements must be made on what is achieved in the Gold Cup at Cheltenham; that is, in the case of chasers that have the stamina and the jumping ability to win this supreme test.

The final word in the Arkle v. Desert Orchid debate rests with Fulke Walwyn, one of the greatest of all British National Hunt trainers, who shortly before he died put it all in perspective. He didn't even mention Desert Orchid in the same breath as Golden Miller, Arkle or Mill House.

"Golden Miller and Arkle stand out from the others and I have good reason to know," said Walwyn. "After all, I rode Golden Miller a few times while Arkle was too good for Mill House, a horse I fondly thought would win me a handful of Cheltenham Gold Cups. They were the best but which was the better is quite another matter.

"I don't think you should ever compare horses of different eras. In fact, I don't think you should ever try to. Golden Miller was the top chaser of his time; Arkle was the best of his. It's best left at that.

"But Mill House was so unfortunate to be Arkle's contemporary. If they hadn't happened along at the same period, my horse would have been the one to compare with Golden MIller.

"I suppose you could argue that Golden Miller actually achieved more than Arkle, five Gold Cups against three and a Grand National as well. But I know how good Mill House was – he was very good – so for Arkle to treat him as he did tells you what I think of Tom Dreaper's horse.

"When Mill House beat Arkle in the 1963 Hennessy I thought we were bound to win the Gold Cup with him again the following March. It was a very nasty shock, the biggest shock of my life, in fact, when that didn't happen. I suppose I went on trying to believe Mill House could turn the form round for a while but in the end, of course, I had to accept that Arkle was superior.

"I'm afraid Arkle finally broke that big horse's heart. He was so unlucky to meet Arkle. So very

THOSE CHAMPION TIMES

Richard Dunwoody with the trophy for the Champion Hurdle after Kribensis's victory at the 1990 Festival meeting.

Ed Byrne captures in graphic style the smooth partnership between Richard Dunwoody and Kribensis as they win at Wincanton on their way to success in the 'Champion'.

Kribensis (Richard Dunwoody) parading before the 1990 Champion Hurdle and (below) not much in it as (left to right) Beech Road, Past Glories, the grey Kribensis and Nomadic Way (blinkers) come to the last but Kribensis goes on to a decisive win.

Another fine study by Ed Byrne of the power generated by Richard Dunwoody on Kribensis and (below) Michael Stoute in happy mood after the 1990 Champion Hurdle triumph.

Morley Street (Jimmy Frost), white sleeves, powers for glory in the 1991 Smurfit Champion Hurdle with Bradbury Star (E. Murphy), on left, and Nomadic Way (Richard Dunwoody), the runner-up, white spotted cap just behind on rails. (Below left) Morley Street leads over the last from Nomadic Way, pictured right as Richard Dunwoody brought him back into the unsaddling enclosure.

Mark Dwyer on Jodami, the winner (left) and Richard Dunwoody on Rushing Wild (right), the runner-up battle it out at the last in the 1993 Gold Cup and (bottom) Richard Dunwoody on Wonder Man has to be content with second place again as Travado (Jamie Osborne), left, gets in a great jump at the last and, landing running, takes the Waterford Castle Arkle Challenge Trophy at the '93 Festival meeting.

Richard Dunwoody on Ebony Jane, centre, Garamycin (Brendan Sheridan) left, and For William (Kevin O'Brien) jumping the last in the 1993 Harold Clarke Leopardstown Handicap Chase, which saw Garamycin hold Ebony Jane's challenge by half-a-length and (below) Dunwoody with Ollie Hannon (camel coat) and the other connections of Montelado after winning the Tote Festival Bumper (N.H. Flat Race) at the 1992 Festival meeting.

Richard Dunwoody jumping the last on Viking Flagship to easily win the B.M.W. Drogheda Chase at the 1993 Punchestown
Festival meeting and (below) looks to be in a winning position
on Second Schedual, left, coming to the last in the Pierse
Contracting John P. Harty Memorial Chase at the same meeting but Bishops Hall (Graham Bradley) mastered him on the
flat to win by two-and-a-half lengths. Ebony Jane (Charlie
Swan) also in picture was fourth.

unlucky."

Finally, there will always be speculation on whether Richard Dunwoody rode Desert Orchid better than Simon Sherwood – or whether the original partnership was the ideal one.

Trainer David Elsworth would not be drawn on the issue.

"When Simon Sherwood decided to call it a day and we were forced to look for a replacement jockey Dunwoody's name was obviously on the short list," he said. "The owner Richard Burridge was keen on him but there were others to consider. I think Richard got the job because Burridge and myself couldn't agree on the other names but we both felt that Dunwoody had claims which we couldn't ignore.

"However, Simon had been with Dessie during the great years, including that marvellous season when Dessie won the Gold Cup. Everything after that had to be beer as opposed to champagne.

"Richard, I feel, rode Dessie superbly, as I expected him to, but he partnered the horse at a time when the see-saw in Dessie's career had begun to tip the other way. It's a bit like marrying Elizabeth Taylor for the second time, isn't it? I wouldn't know, but I think it's a good comparison.

"I had no fault with Dunwoody in the final years of Dessie's career but you have to say that the best days were over by the time Richard came along."

CHAPTER 10

THE ARKLE OF '89
'HIS CROWNING GLORY'

Davvid 'The Duke' Nicholson had no doubt whatsoever that the Arkle Challenge Trophy at the 1989 Cheltenham Festival meeting represented Richard Dunwoody's "crowning glory" because of the sheer brilliance of the ride he gave Waterloo Boy in winning this event.

Sabin Du Loir, the mount of Peter Scudamore, started 5/4 favourite on the strength of an unbeaten record that season and in actual fact was seeking to complete a five-timer.

On his reappearance at Ascot in November, he had won the Racecall Hurdle by a decisive margin for the second year running, then on his debut over fences at Newton Abbot the following month he led all the way to win unchallenged by thirty lengths. A further convincing win followed at Ascot in January and in his final preparatory race before the Festival meeting, he returned to the same venue on February 8th and pulverised the opposition to win by twenty lengths – yes, twenty lengths – from Waterloo Boy, with Weirpool a further twelve lengths away third.

Waterloo Boy was unbeaten that season up to that Ascot event, having recorded five successive victories, including a win by a distance at

Cheltenham in January when he gave a fine display of jumping as he led from start to finish.

He was still only six when he contested the Arkle at the '89 Festival meeting whereas Sabin Du Loir, who had come late to chasing, was now a ten-year-old. Still there were good judges who rated Martin Pipe's charge 'a natural' and who backed him to beat Waterloo Boy and the rest as if he were the banker of the meeting.

In fact, the Jimmy Fitzgerald-trained Phoenix Gold, ridden by Mark Dwyer, was considered on the day a bigger danger to Sabin Du Loir than Waterloo Boy, going off at 5/1. He had won at Nottingham on his previous outing, scoring by five lengths from Southern Minstrel, who subsequently won the Timeform Chase at Haydock and was allowed take his chance in the Arkle, starting at 9/1. The Arthur Moore-trained Feroda, ridden by Tom Taaffe, was a 20/1 chance.

"I rate the Arkle of 1989 Richard's crowning glory if you like, for he did everything right," was David Nicholson's spontaneous tribute to his No. 1 stable jockey after he had won a magnificent battle by half-a-length from Southern Minstrel and Christ Grant with Sabin Du Loir a length further behind third.

"After the way Sabin Du Loir had beaten him at Ascot in his previous run, Richard decided to stick to him throughout the race. He even lined up beside him at the tapes!

"Once the race was under way, he was never more than a length adrift and he put in one of the best finishes I have ever seen, to withstand the challenge of Southern Minstrel from the last, having already seen to it that Sabin Du Loir was not going to dictate matters. What a performance."

In the aftermath of that victory Richard Dunwoody was inclined to shrug it off as "just another race" but tactically he had been brilliant in the way he pressed Sabin Du Loir all the way. 'Scu's mount had been accustomed in all his races over fences that season to going off in front and not knowing really what it was to be challenged and hassled.

Little wonder that 'The Duke' Nicholson enthused to the point that he was willing to tell the racing world: "I regard Dunwoody as the best jump jockey since the Second World War. He has style, nerve and tremendous will to win. I have seen no better – and I am including John Francome in that."

The trainer could be excused perhaps for going over the top somewhat and, remember, that tribute was paid before Dunwoody left the Nicholson stable in '93 to become No. 1 jockey to Martin Pipe after the retirement of Peter Scudamore – and before 'The Duke' had assessed the qualities of Adrian Maguire and stepped in to sign him up as his No. 1 in succession to Dunwoody.

The '89 judgement on Dunwoody was tempered four years later by the amazing impact that Maguire had made in a comparatively short time riding in Britain and Nicholson had to admit that, not alone is he a "very good horseman" but he added that "to do what he has done in that space of time (three years) is phenomenal – better than any recent jockey, be it Francome, Scudamore or Dunwoody. None of them had ridden 125 winners in their third or fourth seasons."

But Nicholson would obviously retain very

happy memories of the partnership Dunwoody and himself enjoyed over "seven marvellous seasons."

The Master of Jackdaws Castle was happy that the 1993 split with Dunwoody was amicable and that they both remained on good terms. And he acknowledged that if it were to happen on a big occasion that Adrian Maguire was going somewhere else, Dunwoody would be his first choice – if it were possible for him to book him.

The 1990 Cheltenham Festival meeting, as we have seen, meant that Dunwoody, by winning the Champion Hurdle on Kribensis, completed the treble of National Hunt racing that every top rider aspires to achieve before he retires. Thus he joined Fred Winter, who won three Champions on Clair Soleil (1955), Fare Time (1959) and Eborneezer (1961), two Gold Cups on Saffron Tartan (1961) and Mandarin (1962) and two Nationals on Sundew (1957) and Kilmore (1962) and Bobby Beasley, who won the Champion on Another Flash (1960), the Gold Cup twice on Roddy Owen (1959) and Captain Christy (1974) and the National on Nicolaus Silver (1961).

Pat Taaffe won the Gold Cup four times (Arkle, 1964-'66 and Fort Leney, 1968) and the National twice (Quare Times, 1955 and Gay Trip, 1970) but missed out on the Champion, though he was second on Ivy Green in 1959 and third on Flyingbolt in 1966.

At that 1990 Festival meeting there seemed every reason to believe on the Tuesday evening that by Thursday night Richard Dunwoody would be acclaimed for emulating Fred Winter's feat of 1961 when he won the Champion Hurdle

(Eborneezer) and Gold Cup (Saffron Tartan) at the same Festival meeting.

But Norton's Coin put paid to the realisation of that dream . . .

However, Dunwoody figured in another epic on the Wednesday on Waterloo Boy and there are Cheltenham regulars, who have not missed the great annual Festival since 1946, who would rate the 1990 battle for the Queen Mother Champion Chase one of the finest races at the venue in modern times, though it must be said that it might have been eclipsed by the three way battle between Remittance Man, Katabatic and Waterloo Boy in the 1992 Champion Chase.

The Hon. George Lambton in his famous work *Men And Horses I Have Known,* writing about the epic race between Sceptre and Ard Patrick for the Eclipse Stakes of 1902, had this to say: "About;the best thing in racing is when two good horses single themselves out from the rest of the field and have a long drawn-out struggle."

Lambton might well have been describing the way Barnbrook Again and Waterloo Boy singled themselves out from the rest of the field and got locked in a never-to-be-forgotten battle from the last fence, Hywel Davies fighting back on Barnbrook Again to edge Waterloo Boy and Dunwoody out of it by a mere half-a-length. In defeat, Nicholson exclaimed: "You won't see a better race than that."

Barnbrook Again was the reigning champion chaser over two miles, having won this race authoritatively by four lengths the previous year and Waterloo Boy, of course, had taken the Arkle Challenge Trophy in 1989. So everything was set for a mouth-watering contest.

Barnbrook Again, the 11/10 favourite, took up the running three fences out but Dunwoody hit the front on Waterloo Boy approaching the last and at that stage seemed set for victory. However, Barnbrook Again, who had been campaigning over three miles, had the edge in stamina when the whips were produced in a grand-stand finish between Davies and Dunwoody and rallied up that punishing hill to be in front where it mattered – the winning post.

Both jockeys were suspended for "excessive use of the whip" and this sparked off yet another storm of controversy over a subject which has been a running sore ever since the Jockey Club in the eyes of many aficionados of the game, began taking more note of the television viewers than the professionals in racing.

In a way it all went back to Cheltenham '80 when the Irish jockeys Tommy Ryan and Joe Byrne were banned for their use of the whip on Drumlargan and Batista. I'll always remember Ryan's comment after coming in on Drumlargan, who had just held on to win the Sun Alliance Novices Hurdle: "There was a lot of money down and I had to win."

At Cheltenham there is a world to win – and lose – when it comes to an all-out battle from the last hurdle or the last fence. A jockey has to try all he knows to get a horse up. If he is lenient and gets narrowly beaten what will the connections say to him, especially if they have their money on at good ante-post odds or have backed him heavily in the ring. And what about the punters who may have "waded in"?

Adrian Maguire didn't avoid using the whip on Cool Ground in the 1992 Gold Cup and, naturally, incurred the wrath of the Stewards but, significantly, Toby Balding wasn't to be found castigating him in public.

French trainer, Francois Doumen had good reason, it can be argued, to complain at the fact that if his jockey Adam Kondrat had been as liberal in the use of the whip, then The Fellow would have turned the tables on Cool Ground.

The Jockeys' Association strongly criticised the Stewards at Cheltenham for being "too stringent" in 1990. Six riders in all received suspension for whip offences that year.

Dealing with the controversy in his column in *Horse and Hound*, Richard Dunwoody expressed disappointment that Hywel Davies and himself had dropped their original intention to appeal. "The appeal, if nothing else, would have exposed once again the inconsistencies of the decisions of Major Steveney,the advising Stipendary in charge, and the Cheltenham Stewards.

"Major Steveney gives the impression he dislikes my style of riding but this should not be allowed to prejudice the style and manner of his questioning at an inquiry.

"Why also were the trainers and the vets not called to give evidence as is usually the case? Guidelines have done a lot of good yet it still remains that one day we can do one thing and be applauded for it and the next day do the very same and have our living taken away. We have got the ridiculous idea of guidelines being interpreted as rules."

Richard Dunwoody got some measure of compensation for the defeats of Waterloo Boy and Desert Orchid at the 1990 Festival meeting when he had a thrilling win on Bigsun for David Nicholson in the Ritz Club National Hunt Chase – the race immediately following the Gold Cup on the Thursday.

Richard got the better of Nigel Hawke in a driving finish to beat Seagram by a head. The same Seagram, would go on to win the Aintree Grand National the following year.

This was vintage Dunwoody. Bigsun, incidentally, was Richard's mount in the Grand National that year and the nine-year-old was a well-backed 15/2 shot. Well in touch for a long way, he was out of contention after the 19th, eventually finishing sixth – but a distant sixth, beaten over 55 lengths by the winner Mr. Frisk, who broke the National record, skipping over the "new" National fences as though they were hurdles. Once again Durham Edition finished second with Rinus third and Brown Windsor, later to become another Dunwoody National mount, in fourth place.

Interestingly enough, Bigsun finished only a length and a half ahead of seventh placed Call Collect, ridden by fellow Ulsterman, the amateur Raymund Martin, cousin of Will who had watched young Dunwoody all those years ago. Raymund had won the Christies Foxhunters on Call Collect the day of Norton's Coin's Gold Cup.

If Waterloo Boy had brought Richard Dunwoody his "crowning glory" in the 1989 Arkle, the same horse also provided him with more than one frustrating narrow defeat, though as in the case of the 1990 Queen Mother Champion Chase, Dunwoody knew that he had helped to add to the lore of truly great races.

This was the case when Nicholson, constant supporter of Irish racing, decided to send Waterloo Boy for the 1989 Black and White Whisky Champion Chase (2½m) at the Leopardstown Christmas meeting.

In the finest race ever for this prize, Waterloo Boy looked the winner jumping the last but, despite the powerful driving of Dunwoody, he was unable to match the superior stamina of John Fowler's Maid Of Money, who ran on under pressure to win by half-a-length. It was obvious that two miles was Waterloo Boy's best trip.

Maid Of Money, who was winning the race for the second year running, went on to have a crack at the Gold Cup but after making a mistake at the seventh was never seen in the race with a chance, finishing a poor sixth.

Nicholson took his defeat at Leopardstown very well and his remark that it was worthwhile coming to Ireland, where you are better treated than in many places in England, went down well with the local professionals.

The season 1989-"90 by no means marked the end of the "Richard Dunwoody/Waterloo Boy Saga".

There were still other rousing battles to come at Cheltenham and elsewhere . . . .

CHAPTER 11

DUNWOODY REACHES HIS
FIRST CENTURY

The 1989-'90 season ended on a high note for Richard Dunwoody. He reached – and passed – the century mark for the first time and actually finished on 102 winners, his best yet.

Although two ahead of Graham McCourt he was still 68 behind Peter Scudamore, who now exerted such a vice-like grip on the title that Dunwoody could hardly be forgiven for pondering the question: Will it ever slacken?

He could not have foreseen then that three years on Scu would suddenly call it a day and, instead of having to battle for his first crown right down to the wire, Dunwoody was assured of the title to all intents and purposes.

Such is life . . .

When Desert Orchid duly won his fourth King George on December 26, 1990 the scenes of euphoria reached such heights at Kempton that another outstanding performance was completely over-shadowed.

Remittance Man, with Dunwoody in the saddle, took the Warners Wayward lad Novices' Chase by twelve lengths, thus maintaining his unbeaten record over the jumps.

Remittance Man emerged as the top novice chas-

131

er of 1990-"91, a season when he won the Arkle Trophy to give Dunwoody yet another big race Cheltenham success. Sadly, however, after another outstanding year in 1991-'92 Remittance Man developed an injury in his off fore tendon after winning at Huntingdon before Christmas 1992 and that put him out for the rest of the season.

Remittance Man's trainer was the Lambourn-based Nicky Henderson, whose name will always be linked with the brilliant See You Then, winner of the Champion Hurdle three years running (1985-'87). Henderson had first claim on Dunwoody's services when he was not required by his retaining stable, David Nicholson's establishment.

Henderson was unstinting in his praise of the Ulsterman when I asked him for his appraisal. "Well, what can you say. He is a superb horseman with a natural gift for getting on with his mounts. But more than that he's the nicest person I know in racing. You just couldn't fall out with him and there are very few like that.

"I would have to rate him with the best. He's certainly as good as John Francome who was the best I ever saw, but what I like about Richard is that he can make a race on a wet Monday at some obscure track appear just as important as one on the big race days. He gives every horse his all and a trainer can fully rely on him.

"You know he rode his 100th winner of the 1992-'93 season on a horse of mine called Grey Hussar at Windsor in February. This was the first time the horse had won but Richard came in as though he had just got off a champion. That's the sort of person he is."

Remittance Man certainly did Henderson proud in 1990-'91 and the gelding did wonders also for Dunwoody's career. He was unbeaten in six chases. And when he came to Cheltenham '91 for the Arkle he had just put in a breathtaking performance the previous month by routing a useful field in the Galloway Braes Novice Chase at Kempton.

In fact, he came home 30 lengths ahead of Monumental Lad, who was receiving 4lbs and who had won his previous race at Huntingdon by 20 lengths while the favourite, File Concord, who was beaten when falling at the final fence, had been a ten-lengths winner on his chasing debut at Warwick in January.

Remittance Man, Uncle Ernie and Last o' The Bunch dominated the betting in the Arkle. While Remittance Man not surprisingly started favourite at 85/40, there was a lot of money for the Jimmy Fitzgerald-trained 5/2 chance Uncle Ernie, the mount of Mark Dwyer. He had gone through the season unbeaten and was actually seeking to complete a six-timer.

Likewise, Last o' The Bunch, trained by Gordon Richards, had set up a sequence of five wins in a row. And while Irish challenger Orbis, ridden by Charlie Swan, went off at 11/1, he arrived at Cheltenham with two successive victories under his belt – the most recent in the Dawn Run Novices Chase at Fairyhouse where he had beaten Garamycin and earlier he had won at Gowran Park.

So the stage was set for a cracker and the followers of Uncle Ernie and Last o' The Bunch could hardly have envisaged that Remittance Man would score so authoritatively in the end.

Richard Dunwoody sent him into the lead three out but momentarily he looked in trouble when Dunwoody produced the whip at the elbow turning into the home straight. However, the persuasive powers – allied to the pressure – of Dunwoody set him alight again, and, although Uncle Ernie looked to be travelling the best of all at the last, Dunwoody got a spectacular leap out of Remittance Man at the last and he pulled away from Jimmy Fitzgerald's charge up the hill to win by a clear six lengths. Last o' The Bunch fell two out and another Irish challenger, Redundant Pal, the mount of Conor O'Dwyer, took third place.

Whereas in 1989 it had been the closeness of the battle between Waterloo boy and Sabin Du Loir which had rivetted the crowd's attention, this time it was the sheer breathtaking excellence of Remittance Man's jumping and power in the finish which held us all spellbound.

The epilogue to that great race was written the following year at Cheltenham when Remittance Man made the Queen Mother Champion Chase his target and it evolved into what the *Irish Racing Annual* described as "A race for the Connoisseurs" in the epic three-way battle between Remittance Man, Katabatic and Waterloo Boy.

But, ironically, Dunwoody, because of his retainer with 'The Duke' Nicholson,had to ride Waterloo Boy and it was Jamie Osborne who had the mount on Remittance Man.

Waterloo Boy had been second in the Queen Mother Champion Chase at Cheltenham '91 to Katabatic, beaten seven lengths, though it had to be said that because of a slight setback he had missed his preparatory race at Kempton in February.

Dunwoody sent Waterloo Boy into the lead on the run to the second last with Remittance Man pressing strongly and Simon McNeill on Katabatic not far behind. Osborne was the first to get to work and Remittance Man responded gamely to take the lead from Waterloo Boy at the last. Katabatic didn't jump the last as fluently as Remittance Man but still landed full of running and with a sustained challenge looked as if he might win it. However, Remittance Man powered strongly up the hill to beat Katabatic by a length with Waterloo Boy three-and-a-half lengths further away in third place.

"Whatever their original allegiance, almost everyone walked away from the finish with stars in their eyes," wrote John Oaksey in the *Daily Telegraph*. "Remittance Man and his courageous rivals had given us the best that National Hunt racing has to offer.

"The sight of three chasers running at full speed and rising close together at the final fence, will not be forgotten for many a year by the 33,551 crowd," was how Richard Evans described the climactic stages in *The Times*, adding: "The roar that greeted not only Jamie Osborne and Remittance Man, but also the gallant placed horses, was close to Desert Orchid proportions."

Little wonder then that the atmosphere around the unsaddling enclosure was very special and evocative.

And while Remittance Man had fittingly justified evens favouritism, David Nicholson, gracious as ever and among the first to congratulate Nicky

Henderson, could still feel proud of Waterloo Boy and the ride that Richard Dunwoody had given him. Prouder still that his charge had contributed handsomely to the making of a classic of National Hunt racing. As he put it: "We were lucky to play a part in a great race."

But to Cheltenham '91 . . .

Dunwoody had every reason to look forward to winning the Sun Alliance Novices Chase on the Wednesday on Nicky Henderson's Sparkling Flame, who had shown immense promise on his debut at Lingfield in December '90 and then at the Kempton Christmas meeting had a fifteen lengths' win in the Butlin's Feltham Novices Chase (3m), Dunwoody making his challenge approaching the last and experiencing no difficulty in beating Ardbrin.

George Stewart from Lisburn, Co. Antrim, trained Sparkling Flame in his point to point days and the gelding always looked destined for the top, winning three times like a future champion.

Sparkling Flame fell in the Sun Alliance and Dunwoody had to wait until the Liverpool Grand National meeting for his next success on this talented gelding.

The race was the Mumm Club Novices Chase and Sparkling Flame slammed Esha Ness by eight lengths. This was reckoned by *Timeform* to be the best performance of the season by a staying novice chaser, for Esha Ness had been runner-up in the Sun Alliance and Sparkling Flame gave him six pounds at Liverpool. The future seemed bright for Sparkling Flame but a set-back in training was looming around the corner.

It was at the time of Sparkling Flame's Aintree

win that Dunwoody began to look like the new champion.

In November 1990 Peter Scudamore had run into the sort of accident all jump jockeys dread – a broken leg.

He was on a horse trained by Charlie Brooks called Black Humour of all things, and Scudamore must have thought this was an ironic appellation in view of the pain he went through in the weeks that followed.

"The meeting was Market Rasen and I was riding in a hurdle race," he told me. "Black Humour hit the top of a hurdle and seemed to take a long time to come down. Anyway, I stayed with the horse when I would have been better off thrown clear and as a result the horse fell on top of me. I had no idea I had broken a leg until I tried to get up again."

That injury gave Dunwoody his chance and, although he and Scudamore are the best of friends, Richard knew that he had to take advantage of Scu's misfortune.

So he pressed on and was leading the champion ship by 20 – seemingly unassailable – when Scudamore made his come-back at the end of January, and proceeded to ride a winner that day.

"The meeting was Newton Abbot," Scu said, "and I scored on Outside Edge who ironically was bred in Northern Ireland by Jeremy Maxwell. This win gave me the incentive to go on and after that it was hammer-and-tongs for the title, although to be honest I wasn't really thinking about the championship then. I was just hoping to ride winners when I could and stay in one piece."

Dunwoody knew he had a fight on his hands

but he held his lead until May when Scudamore swept to the top of the table and after that Dunwoody realised that the odds were against him reaching his life's ambition that season.

Earlier in the year Dunwoody had made no secret of the fact that he was grimly determined to win the title. "I'd give anything to be champion jockey," he said when he was down to a precarious two in front at the beginning of May. And this after months of bone-breaking risk and 40,000 miles of driving to places as "exotic" as Perth and Southwell.

At the back end of his mind, however, was the thought that he might suffer the same injuries as Scudamore and he had one minor fright when he lost a week at the New Year through a neck injury and a mouthful of chipped teeth. But really this is small beer to jump jockeys. They are made of sterner stuff and Dunwoody barely noticed his injuries.

After Scudamore had bounced back and begun to catch Dunwoody, Richard remarked in April that he felt his great rival would be successful in the end.

"He has all the Martin Pipe horses which will keep going until the last day of the season. My main trainers, David Nicholson and Nicky Henderson are doing their best but they just haven't that sort of ammunition," he said.

This was painfully obvious to Dunwoody as he watched the incredible Pipe bandwagon roll remorselessly on through May like Hitler's Panzers had done through France and Belgium fifty-one years earlier.

Even so, Dunwoody refused to give up. His rare

quality of a mixture of courageous naivety and calculation makes him the jockey he is, the man for the big occasion and he has always had the ability to make the difficult seem easy.

He certainly had his work cut out in the closing weeks of 1990-'91 and his remark near the end of the campaign: "I'll go anywhere for a ride for the title means a hell of a lot to me," had a somewhat poignant ring.

But it was not to be.

You couldn't help feeling sorry for Dunwoody at the end of a memorable year. He had reached the heights on the best horses in England, like Desert Orchid and Remittance Man, but at the end of the day the man who had the power of the Pipe stable behind him as the winners flowed at places like Newton Abbot, Taunton and Devon and Exeter with extraordinary frequency came out on top.

I remember hearing a punter observe when he was informed that the next day's card lacked class: "That may be so but there are still going to be six winners."

Peter Scudamore would have seconded that as he was crowned champion yet again.

The final irony for Richard Dunwoody lay in the fact that he had his best-ever season, finishing with a tally of 127 winners – only 14 behind Scudamore.

Yes, the gap was closing but a disappointed Dunwoody must have felt that the championship title had been agonisingly snatched from his grasp that same season after he had looked a winner for so long.

His time would come.

CHAPTER 12

'JUST ANOTHER JOB'

"To me it was just another job." In this one seven-word sentence Richard Dunwoody summed up the situation when he was asked to take over the riding of Morley Street after owner Michael Jackson had jocked off Jimmy Frost in controversial circumstances.

"I hadn't ridden for Toby Balding but I was looking forward to the challenge on Morley Street," Richard went on. "Of course, I felt sorry for Jimmy Frost who had done nothing wrong as far as I was concerned and I must say there was no animosity between us. We remained the best of friends."

Richard Dunwoody was taking the born professionals' approach. He had not sought the ride on Morley Street. He had not cut inside Jimmy Frost. He realised that once a breach had come in the relationship between Michael Jackson as the owner and Jimmy Frost as the jockey, then it was obvious that Jackson was going to look elsewhere for a new rider. If Dunwoody did not accept the offer, then it would obviously go to someone else. That was the bottom line.

Morley Street, a full brother of Granville Again, first burst on the scene as a possible winner of the Champion Hurdle when he thrashed the opposition in the Mumm Prize Novices' Hurdle (2½ miles) – the last race on the card – at Liverpool on Grand National Day '89. In completing a treble that day for Toby Balding, who had already won the Sandeman Aintree Hurdle with Beech Road and the Grand National with Little Polveir, Morley Street came home one-and-a-half lengths ahead of the 3/1 favourite Trapper John, ridden by Tommy Carmody.

In the hands of Jimmy Frost on that occasion, Morley Street jumped into the lead at the last and ran on too strongly for the opposition.

So the stage seemed set for a very successful campaign the following season.

Second on his re-appearance at Newbury in November '89, he stripped much fitter next time out at Cheltenham on December 9 and, leading at the last in the Mercury Communications Hurdle (2½ miles), he quickened impressively to put seven lengths between himself and Deep Sensation, who was ridden by Richard Dunwoody. Morley Street started 4/7 favourite that day.

Waiting tactics were best on Morley Street and it was clear that he could not be shown daylight too soon. Indeed, if he took the lead too early he would idle in front and be "done" by a late-finishing rival.

This is exactly what happened in Morley Street's next race – the Racing International Hurdle at Chepstow on December 23. Installed the 8/13 favourite in a field of eight, he found himself in the lead three out but once they cleared the last, Jimmy Frost was forced to go for his whip as Morley Street began to idle and, in fact, in the closing stages the 11/1 shot Propero got up to beat him by

142

three-quarters-of-a-length.

He didn't run again until the Champion Hurdle for which he started 10/1 with stable companion, Beech Road the 2/1 favourite to repeat his success in this race at the 1989 Festival meeting. It was noticeable that Morley Street sweated up during the preliminaries and on the fast going that day, he found the pace too fast for him over this distance and some professional race-readers concluded that he might be best over 2½ miles against a field of 'Champion' class.

He finished fifth behind Kribensis and Richard Dunwoody, as he came back into the winner's enclosure, could hardly have imagined that by the Spring of 1992,he would have become the rider of Morley Street.

At the 1990 Aintree Grand National meeting, Morley Street came back to form with a bang, winning the Sandeman Aintree Hurdle (2½ miles) in a common canter by fifteen lengths from Joyful Noise at levels.

The following season he was put to chasing and a win in the Breeders Cup at Fair Hill seemed to indicate that his future might lie over the bigger obstacles. On his English debut over fences at Worcester on December 3, 1990,he won comfortably, despite carrying a penalty for his American success. His next outing was in a novice chase (2½ miles) at Ascot where he finished second to Remittance Man, and although he was beaten eight lengths, the overall achievements of Remittance Man proved that it was far better form than might have appeared to be the case on the surface.

Morley Street was installed 13/8 favourite to win the Butlin's Feltham Novices's Chase at

Kempton on December 26. However, after he had been pulled up before the third last, it was found that he had burst a blood vessel and Toby Balding took the immediate decision that he would revert to a hurdling programme. Incidentally, the winner of that Kempton chase was Sparkling Flame, ridden by Richard Dunwoody for Nicky Henderson – so Dunwoody's path was continuing to cross that of Morley Street.

Balding's decision was rewarded when Morley Street returned to winning form in the Berkshire Hurdle on March 1st – his final preparatory race before the Champion Hurdle, for which he would start 4/1 favourite, with his regular rider, Jimmy Frost in the saddle.

The yielding going was all in his favour that day and, although he took the lead after the second last, he maintained his run over the last. Despite edging right in the climb to the finish, he did not falter and held the strong challenge of Nomadic Way and Richard Dunwoody by a length-and-a-half.

When Morley Street produced another effortless success in winning the Sandeman Aintree Hurdle for the second year running – this time confirming his superiority over Nomadic Way by six lengths – there seemed little doubt that he could win the Champion Hurdle again in 1992 and probably make a bold bid for the three-timer in '93.

But all would go terribly wrong during the 1991-'92 campaign – especially for Jimmy Frost.

There was nothing on the horizon to indicate this when Morley Street travelled to Belmont Park, New York in October and won the Breeders Cup for the second successive year.

Back over hurdles for the Racecall Ascot Hurdle in November, he looked to be coasting in at one stage but once he was in front, the exasperating habit of idling revealed itself and it was only by a neck that he beat King's Curate in the end.

Installed 8/11 favourite for the Paschal Butler Champion Hurdle at Leopardstown on February 1st, he looked to have victory wrapped up when he led over the last but again he began to idle in front and was caught on the line and beaten a short-head by the 20/1 chance Chirkpar from the Jim Bolger stable.

The question, of course, was: had Jimmy Frost come too soon? It could be argued that Frost, knowing he had a double handful, could have waited and waited and wouldn't have been "done". Yet, in the Champion Hurdle the previous year, Morley Street, as we have seen, led over the last – and didn't get caught and no one was blaming Frost that day., or later at Liverpool for that matter. Defeat, however, inevitably brings recriminations and raises questions.

There is little doubt that Morley Street was a top-class hurdler but a frustrating one in the sense that he could fail when most was expected of him. He was a firm favourite to retain his crown in the 1992 Champion Hurdle, going off at 2/1 after opening at 3/1. Next best in the market was his full brother, Granville Again at 9/2.

Royal Gait, with little experience over hurdles, had won a lot of admirers by his victory at Nottingham the previous month and there was a lot of "inspired" money for him in the ring, which saw 4/1 taken before he eventually started at 6/1.

The going was good this time and whether this

was a contributory factor to Morley Street's downfall we will never know. The fact of the matter was that Jimmy Frost made his bid approaching the second last and obviously if Morley Street was going to give a repeat of his '91 performance,he would at least have finished in the frame as 20/1 chance. Oh So Risky eventually finished second, beaten half-a-length,to Royal Gait while another 20/1 chance, Ruling was third, another short head away, followed by Fidway with the 50/1 shot Bank View in fifth place just ahead of Morley Street.

No, the form was too bad to be true in Morley Street's case.

Jimmy Frost became the fall guy for this defeat. Michael Jackson seemed to have decided that he was yesterday's man as far as he was concerned and nothing was going to deter him from opting for another rider. The call went out for Richard Dunwoody.

Reflecting on how he lost the ride on Morley Street, Jimmy Frost had this to say to me at the end of the 1992-'93 season: "I felt I was unfairly jocked off Morley Street but I bear no grudge against Richard (Dunwoody). It wasn't his fault and I regard him as a fine horseman. He has all the good qualities and I wish him well for future championships. With Martin Pipe's horses behind him he should be on top of the pile for a long time to come.

"However, I still don't understand why I was taken off Morley Street after the 1992 Champion Hurdle for I had won 15 times on the horse and had also scored in two Breeder's Cups as well as the 1991 Champion. When we were sixth behind Royal Gait in '92 I was only riding the horse the way I had always done.

"The owners decision which was communicated to me through the trainer appeared to be based purely on tha tone race so I was surprised as well as disappointed. But you can't expect tourture hard feelings in this game.

"I must say Graham Bradley gave him a great ride when he won at Liverpool in 1993 after Richard Dunwoody had been claimed by Nicky Henderson for Flown."

Ironically, there was very nearly egg left on Michael Jackson's face – in a big way – when it came to Morley Street making his bid for the Martell Aintree Hurdle – the race he had won by six lengths the previous year.

Now with Dunwoody in the saddle, and starting 4/5 favourite, he looked a "good thing" as he strode clear between the last two hurdles and all that seemed at issue was how many lengths he would be in front at the post.

But again he idled. Tony Mullins got to work on Minorettes Girl, trained by his father at Goresbridge, County Kilkenny and the mare responded in very game fashion to keep reducing the leeway all the way to the line, failing in the end by only half-a-length.

All credit to Dunwoody for ensuring that Morley Street did not toss victory away but even he would accept that it was almost too close for comfort and inwardly he must have had cause to sympathise with Jimmy Frost when he contemplated the kind of frustration that Morley Street, considering his ability, could visit on anyone riding him – and on the connections in general.

The epilogue to the "Morley Street Story" is that

when he won this Aintree race again in '93, beating Granville Again, winner of the '93 'Champion' by one-and-a-half-lengths with Flown third and Ruling fourth, Richard Dunwoody was no longer with him. Graham Bradley, while joining Granville Again at the last, continued to hold Morley Street up to the very last second and it was as late as possible that he kicked on – and in quickening, proved too good on the day for 'Granville'.

'Make it the late, late show' . . . that seemed to be the ideal motto when riding Morley Street.

Anyway, back on December 12th, '92, Richard Dunwoody's faith in Morley Street as a Champion Hurdle proposition at the Festival meeting in '93 had begun to wane. He started 15/8 that day for the Arlington Bula Hurdle, with Granville Again the 7/4 favourite. But both crashed to Halkapous, the mount of Adrian Maguire. He came home ten lengths ahead of Granville Again with Morley Street third. (Morley Street did beat Granville Again at Cheltenham's December Sunday meeting and Dunwoody was suitably enthusiastic, telling me: "What class. He has more gears than any other I've seen.")

But at Sandown in the Agfa Hurdle on February 6th, '93, Morley Street was a big disappointment, finishing fifth to 33/1 chance Mole Board and the distances at the finish read: "6, 20, 15, dist."

Even though Dunwoody showed him the whip, he could get no response from him and he had almost come to a standstill on the run-in.

"Come home Jimmy Frost, all is forgiven . . .", might well have been the catch-cry of the day.

Richard Dunwoody opted for the Nicky Henderson-trained Flown as his mount in the 1993

148

Champion Hurdle on the strength of this one's 30-length triumph in the 'National Spirit' Challenge Trophy Hurdle at Fontwell the previous month. But it had to be noted that his two principal rivals, Dancing Paddy and Masai Mara both fell at the second last, so the form had to be suspect.

Flown, however, started 7/2 favourite for the 'Champion' and, while he appeared to be going quite well at the second last, he could pull out nothing when asked for his effort by Richard Dunwoody and was a major disappointment on the day that Morley Street's brother, Granville Again made it a fitting farewell to the Festival scene for Peter Scudamore – though we did not know it then – by taking the race from Royal Derbi and Halkapous.

"The race was run to suit me and I haven't any excuses," said Dunwoody afterwards. But it was noticeable that Flown began to swish his tail when he drew level with the leaders.

Let's now return to that 1992 Cheltenham Festival meeting when Dunwoody entered the Morley Street picture. He had no mount in the Gold Cup that year, as Desert Orchid had been retired after falling in last place at the third last when bidding for a five-timer in the 'King George'. In a way it was a sad exit, for the grey had been accorded an unforgettable reception as he appeared on the course and when he put in a great jump to lead at the third, his supporters thought that it would be another epoch-making occasion. However, after he had lost the lead at the fifth, he made a bad mistake at the eleventh which put paid to his chance and after that the writing was on the wall for the 'people's champion'.

The race was won in brilliant style by the Francois Doumen-trained The Fellow, who beat Wayward Lad's course record, set in 1983, by over a second.

Still Dunwoody came away from the '92 Festival meeting with two winners, namely Thetford Forest, which won the Sun Alliance Novices Hurdle for 'The Duke' Nicholson and Montelado, who scored an 8/1 surprise in the Tote Festival Bumper and in the process thwarted a major gamble by the Irish contingent on the apparent 'bet of the meeting' in Tiananmen Square. Dunwoody cleverly slipped his field three furlongs out and had the race won before amateur Tim Hyde got Tiananmen Square going – but at the post twelve lengths separated them. Incidentally, Tiananmen Square subsequently reversed the placings at the Punchestown Festival meeting.

Brown Windsor from the Nicky Henderson stable was Richard Dunwoody's mount in the 1992 Aintree Grand National – a gelding Richard had ridden many times but who hadn't raced during the 1990-'91 season, having been pin-fired following his last race of the previous season.

In that successful season Brown Windsor had finished a good fourth in Mr. Frisk's National after having won the Cathcart Cup at Cheltenham, and as a previous winner at Aintree and also of the Whitbread Gold Cup at Sandown he gave every indication that he would be the right sort for future Nationals.

Dunwoody, of course, hadn't ridden him in the 1990 National, but he had in most of his other major outings. And it was after one of these early races that Dunwoody fell foul of the stewards once more.

This was after the Mandarin Chase at Newbury in December 1989 when Brown Windsor was a strong finishing runner-up to Polyfemus. A video re-run of the race showed Dunwoody appearing to hit Brown Windsor 19 times from the second last fence and the vet reported to the Stewards afterwards that Brown Windsor was marked but not injured.

Dunwoody picked up a two-days' suspension but ironically he had been banned for three days by the Irish Stewards earlier in the week for not trying hard enough on the Mick O'Toole-trained Fourth of July at Leopardstown!

"I would rather not comment but rules are rules," said Dunwoody, and this has been his policy throughout most of his encounters with the Stewards, with the exception of that major confrontation following the Barnbrook Again/Waterloo Boy affair at Cheltenham three months later.

Brown Windsor only scored one win in the 1991-'92 season and that was in a handicap chase at Sandown in March. In his other runs he appeared to have lost the sparkle of earlier years, but because of the fact that he had run well on his previous visit to Aintree and his undoubted class he was made second favourite for the National.

Would he bring Dunwoody back into the winners enclosure escorted by those almost legendary mounted policemen? Sadly, it was not to be for Brown Windsor was one of the early casualties, running into another horse and coming down at Bechers first time round when lying second. He also ran in the Whitbread – again starting favourite

– but weakened quickly after a mistake at the 17th fence.

On the opening day of that '92 Liverpool meeting Dunwoody had ridden Carobee for the Nicholson stable in the Seagram Top Novices' Hurdle, the opening event on the card. Flown was the 13/8 favourite with Carobee at 2/1 and Halkapous at 11/4.

Carobee, a fifteen-lengths winner at Chepstow on his previous run, certainly caught the eye that day and confidently ridden by Dunwoody, he beat Halkapous by four lengths, with Flown fourth.

Trainer David Nicholson could hardly contain himself in the Press interviews afterwards. "He's the best horse I have ever trained and you have just seen a future Gold Cup winner. He's better than Broadsword or Very Promising and in my view he has a marvellous future," said 'The Duke'.

Dunwoody agreed that he had been on the bridle for most of the race and, although Richard is never expansive in his tributes, it was obvious from his demeanour that a nod was as good as a wink in this case.

Carobee, then, looked a future star for he was winning his fifth race from six starts. Unfortunately, however, as appears to be the case with so many good horses these days, he too met with a setback and was taken out of training the following season.

It turned out to be a good Liverpool for Dunwoody in '92 for not only did Carobee win, Richard also scored a highly impressive success on Remittance Man who showed all his old sparkle to win the Mumm Melling Chase from Edberg and have Nicky Henderson waxing lyrical afterwards about the following year's Gold Cup.

Dunwoody also scored for Gordon Richards on The Antartex in the John Hughes Memorial Chase, maintaining his remarkable record in this race which he had also won not only on Glen Rue but on Nicky Henderson's Won't Be Gone Long in 1990.

Remittance Man and Waterloo Boy were the horses that helped Richard Dunwoody command the headlines again and again during that season.

Waterloo Boy in particular gave Dunwoody many memorable rides, after having been hob-dayed during the summer.

He won the Tingle Creek Chase at Sandown, the Castleford Chase at Wetherby, the Victor Chandler at Ascot and the Game Spirit at Newbury with, by common consent, his best performance coming in the Victor Chandler.

Once again his old rival Young Snugfit provided the main opposition at Ascot and with a three pounds pull in the weights compared to Sandown, he appeared to have every chance of success.

Young Snugfit set a cracking gallop but after looking as if he had been held between the last two fences, Waterloo Boy staged a grandstand finish to forge ahead in the last 100 yards to win by two lengths.

At Newbury on Tote Gold Trophy Hurdle day the public had the chance to see the two main two-mile contenders in action, as Remittance Man, after having flopped in the King George at Kempton over three miles, was brought back to two and a half miles for the Arlington Premier Chase final, while Waterloo Boy ran in the recognised trial for the Queen Mother at Cheltenham, the Game Spirit

Chase.

With Dunwoody up, Waterloo Boy duly obliged, drawing clear from the last to beat Uncle Ernie by four lengths at level weight but his performance didn't begin to compare with that of Remittance Man in the Arlington.

Although with the defection of Rolling Ball the opposition was not as good as it might have been, the style of Remittance Man's win was something to savour. Again ridden by Dunwoody, he made light of the fences and his apparently effortless 20-lengths win from Captain Dibble marked him down as a banker bet for the Queen Mother for which he was being aimed instead for the Gold Cup.

It turned out to be a race for 'The Connoisseurs', as we have already seen, one of the finest chases seen at the Festival meeting in modern times.

Richard Dunwoody ended the 1991-'92 season on 137 winners but Peter Scudamore was still light years ahead on 175.

It seemed that the gap would never close. But those who saw Scu continuing to hold the title for a number of years to come were in for a rude awakening.

Dunwoody started the 1992-'93 campaign in whirlwind fashion and by the time Christmas arrived, he began to look the clear favourite to win his first crown.

Into January and the odds shortened further as Dunwoody approached 20 clear of his main rival. And there were no injuries involved. He was just getting more winners than Scudamore whose main supplier, Martin Pipe, was not hitting the heights in customary fashion.

"To be honest I was prepared to give up the thought of retaining the title around Christmas time," Scudamore told me. "I didn't see how I could catch Richard."

But then the tide began to turn and from looking good, Dunwoody started to appear like Morley Street. He was in front but couldn't increase his lead.

Slowly but surely the gap began to close so that by February, Dunwoody was only five ahead as Scu began to get them in handfuls while Dunwoody started to falter.

Fair enough, he reached his fastest ever 100 winners in February thanks to Nicky Henderson, but it was the lack of sufficient firing power from the Lambourn stable which was hindering the Dunwoody progress.

Nicholson had been having a marvellous season but he couldn't be expected to continue his high strike rate for ever. Dunwoody needed the other part of his double retainer – and it wasn't coming along as quickly as he would have liked.

Three major setbacks also affected Richard's fight for the championship. First of all Remittance Man, who must have been his banker, was injured at Huntingdon in November and was later pronounced out for the season. Then the enigmatic Morley Street began to disappoint again.

The worst blow of all, however, occurred on January 30 at Cheltenham when Mighty Mogul, who looked a certain winner of the Champion Hurdle, received a fracture and a chip off the off-fore knee and was put down following an operation.

Mighty Mogul, who had been bred by Richard

Morrow at Dundonald, near Belfast – the man who had also bred 1992 Cheltenham winner MIller Hill – was with Jenny Pitman before leaving that stable and going to Nicholson where he soon became ante-post favourite for the Champion.

Before that fateful Cheltenham race, Mighty Mogul had proved virtually unbeatable,running up five wins, and Nicholson was beginning to look to his first Champion success. But all turned to ashes.

"Why is it that only the good horses appear to run into serious injury?" I asked 'The Duke'.

"Because they give you so much," was the poignant reply.

For Dunwoody, coming on top of Remittance Man's misfortune it was a shattering blow, for horses that might have been viewed as "bankers" in adding to his seasonal total had now fallen by the wayside and he had to concentrate more on searching for mounts from any quarter and races in every corner of Britain to win that title. Yes, no longer could he bank on the cream to boost his score. He had to start getting accustomed to a more stable diet.

Once again Fate stepped in – as it had done so at earlier moments in Dunwoody's career – and in one sweep he found himself, instead of struggling desperately to gain the coveted crown, having it literally handed to him on a plate . . . by a decision entirely outside his control.

CHAPTER 13

EXIT 'SCU' – AND
DUNWOODY IS CHAMPION

T he 1993 Festival meeting had come and gone
and then four days after the "Grand National
that never was" Peter Scudamore announced
to a stunned racing world that he had decided to
retire from the saddle.

In one stroke he virtually handed the Jockeys'
Championship title to Richard Dunwoody on a
plate.

At the time the race for the crown was on with a
vengeance. Dunwoody was seventeen ahead but
with two-and-a-half months still to go to the end of
the season, who was to say what would have happened.

Indeed, Dunwoody knew that once his main stables closed up shop for the season, the winners
would still be rolling off the "Pipe line" and there
was every possibility that he would be "done"
again at the finish.

No one but Scudamore's wife Marilyn and closest friends know the reasons why he suddenly
decided to step down.

"I have had enough," was all he would say at
the time.

The fact remains that those who had seen him in
the days leading up to his fateful announcement

noted how tired and haggard he looked. Here was a man who had given his all, season after season, in the relentless hunt for winners and the retention of his title. There must come a moment when one who has achieved it all – and more – has got to decide between further glory and the risks involved to health and limbs, not overlooking either, family considerations.

You could go a bridge too far – and Scu was not prepared to do that.

Furthermore, he had found when he suffered a broken leg a few seasons previously that he had an earning power outside of race riding. His immense popularity made him a big hit in the sphere of television appearances, newspaper columnist and generally using his name and his image.

It was not going to be a case then of his earning capacity drying up completely once he decided to call it a day. No, Scu would continue to be very much part of the National Hunt scene.

Richard Dunwoody echoed the feelings of Scu's fellow-jockeys and, indeed, the vast body of racing followers when he said: "Racing will take a long time to recover from Scu's retirement. Personally, it came as a severe shock to me. We will miss him in the weigh room and I have no idea what prompted his decision. John Francome was the first man I respected and after that there was Scu. There will never be another like him.

"Although we were rivals for the championship, there was never any animosity between us. In fact, we were always willing to help each other.

"You know, he played his cards close to his chest when it came to his retirement. There wasn't a whimper about it beforehand, even after we discussed the National mix-up. I knew nothing until I read it in the paper for which he writes. But then that's the way to handle an exclusive, isn't it?"

Dunwoody acknowledged that as for the championship, suddenly the pressure was off him and what remained for him in the closing stages of the season was to finish with as many winners as possible. "I am looking at the 160 mark but when you consider that Scu rode 60 more than that in his best season, you have some idea of his great talent. What a loss."

Scu's retirement and all that stemmed from it lay ahead of Dunwoody when he contemplated the bag of winners that the Cheltenham and Aintree meetings looked like bringing him.

He had every reason to feel confident that Cheltenham '93 would see him net the Ritz Club Trophy as David Nicholson appeared to have a very strong hand with Baydon Star in the Stayers Hurdle, Wonder Man in the Arkle Trophy and Waterloo Boy in the Champion Chase. And with good ground appearing to be the order of the day, there were high hopes that Nicky Henderson's Flown would take wings in the Champion Hurdle.

Cheltenham and Liverpool have always had a special significance for Dunwoody. He looks forward to both with a rising sense of anticipation, savouring the challenge and the glory that each can bring.

Cheltenham, of course, dwarfs every other meeting in the National Hunt calendar. "It's the Mecca after all," is how he puts it simply.

The Festival meeting of '93 wasn't as kind to him in the final analysis as he had anticipated – just one lone success – but he could say to me:

"Cheltenham still gives me a buzz. Fair enough, I didn't have a great meeting this time but I'm not disappointed. It's a tremendous three days racing and with the opposition so hot, you must expect to get beaten even when you are on fancied ones."

Cheltenham proved once again that it is a law unto itself. Instead of Dunwoody justifying favouritism by taking the Ritz Club Trophy and being acclaimed as the jockey of the meeting, it was Charlie Swan, the Irish champion National Hunt rider, who stole the limelight and the Ritz Club Trophy by riding four winners over the three days.

Laid-back Charlie made it look all so easy and Irish trainers struck gold by scooping six winners, including three on the final day.

Dunwoody's much-vaunted mounts failed to rise to the occasion and, embarrassingly for such an accomplished rider, he had to wait until the very last race, the County Hurdle, before coming good on Nicky Henderson's Thumbs Up, a horse previously trained in Dunwoody's native Ulster by Billy Rock in Cullybackey, County Antrim and whose first win was in a bumper at Down Royal.

Before the eclipse of Flown in the Champion Hurdle – a case of "one up for Scu" – Dunwoody had got close on Wonder Man in the Arkle Trophy but he had the chagrin all the same of being beaten on Nicholson's horse by one from the Nicky Henderson stable, Travado, who got up in the hands of Jamie Osborne to win by a length.

Then Waterloo Boy flopped in the Queen Mother Champion Chase, Deep Sensation just getting the better of Scu on the Martin Pipe-trained Cyphrate. Where was Waterloo Boy? After making an effort four out he weakened rapidly and was virtually pulled up on the run in.

For Scu it was an even better day than the opening afternoon for he followed up Granville Again's victory in the Champion Hurdle by landing a double on Young Hustler in the Sun Alliance Chase and Olympian in the Coral Cup Handicap Hurdle. However, he chose Chatam in the following day's Gold Cup and that was to prove to be a move which almost let his old rival in for a second triumph in the Cheltenham showpiece.

Rushing Wild, also from the Pipe stable, had been the other serious contender for Scudamore's talented hands and heels but he had been beaten by Country Member at Sandown. And when Country Member was shaded a short head by Givus A Buck in the Ritz Club at Cheltenham, Scu decided to plump for Chatam who after all had been narrowly beaten by Jodami at Leopardstown in the Hennessy Irish Gold Cup and Jodami was reckoned to be one of the favourites for the Cheltenham Blue Riband.

Rushing Wild looked like being ridden by Pipe's promising No. 2 Jonathan Lower. But then came an eleventh hour drama. Once again Dunwoody was in centre stage.

David Nicholson decided that the ground was too firm for Another Coral and that left Dunwoody free like a lion released from a cage. He was ready to pounce and it was Rushing Wild who linked up with him when Martin Pipe – later to become even more deeply involved with the Dunwoody talents – made the call.

So Gold Cup day saw Dunwoody riding for Pipe on what was ostensibly the stable's No. 2, but everyone knew that the Ulsterman could conjure up a breathtaking performance from almost any horse. And so it proved with Rushing Wild. Taking the bold approach he made most of the running and kicked clear approaching three out. This policy seemed set to give him the Gold Cup – until Mark Dwyer arrived on the scene with a double handful on Jodami and at the last he jumped upsides Rushing Wild.

Supporters of Dunwoody were hoping that there still might be something left in the tank but if there was then Dwyer had more for he soon drew clear to run on strongly up the hill and beat Dunwoody by a length and a half. A close one then. But not good enough for Dunwoody.

"He jumped super," Dunwoody said afterwards. "I kicked on down the hill to stretch them but Jodami joined me going to the second last and from that point on, he was always going to beat me."

Tragically, Rushing Wild was later put down when suffering a fatal injury in the Jameson Irish Grand National, for which he started joint second favourite, again with Dunwoody in the saddle.

At Cheltenham Dunwoody was forced to pull Barton Bank up in the Sun Alliance Chase when he burst a blood vessel. This was particularly galling for, as he put it, "Barton Bank had been running so well all the season."

With a philosophical shrug of his shoulders, he added: "But what can you do? You must press on to the next hurdle."

Dunwoody's next hurdle was Aintree. But before then he must have had thoughts on the problems involved with having a retainer.

The opening race at Cheltenham, the Trafalgar House Supreme Novices Hurdle, was won by the Pat Flynn-trained Montelado on whom Dunwoody had ben successful the previous year in the Festival Bumper. It was no secret that he would have liked to ride the horse again but Nicholson had that claim on him and he was booked for Dreamer's Delight who fell in the big Cheltenham race.

"There were some who said that I didn't want to ride Montelado and had made the retainer the excuse," Richard told me before Cheltenham. "But that wasn't the case. You have to honour any claim that's made on you and you aren't always free to partner the horse you would have liked to ride."

In view of the problems which were to surround Dunwoody regarding claims only a month later those words were somewhat prophetic.

Anyway it was on to Liverpool. Hopes were high of a win in the National on Nicky Henderson's Won't Be Gone Long with other good mounts in the offing.

But before that Dunwoody encountered one or two hiccups along the way.

Two days after the 'Gold Cup, Dunwoody took a fall at Uttoxeter which at the time seemed innocuous enough but which in fact, cost him some valuable days.

That old spectre of injury is never far away from a National Hunt jockey's mind. Dunwoody, however, had been very fortunate in that 1992-'93 had seen him escape – until Uttoxeter.

Even that fall on his right hand the Saturday after Cheltenham appeared to be nothing serious, but after he had ridden in the first race at Fontwell the following Tuesday,the pain became unbearable and he went to have his hand X-rayed at Chichester Hospital.

A broken bone was discovered but Dunwoody wasn't too put out by the setback. Liverpool was the following week and he felt he still had time to recover.

"It's nothing to worry about," he assured his anxious fans. "I hope to be back either at Sandown next Tuesday – the week of Aintree – or Ascot the following day."

Dunwoody at this time had a 15-winner lead over Scu and with 140 on the board he was in a reasonably confident mood. But he was taking no chances about the meeting. He intended to be at Aintree, and so he rested.

The day after the announcement of the injury Dunwoody saw a specialist in Ridgeway Hospital in Swindon and also received treatment from physiotherapist Mary Bromley.

Afterwards Dunwoody confirmed that his enforced lay-off was due to a broken fourth finger.

Meanwhile, Scu missed a glorious opportunity to cut into Dunwoody's lead – by now down to 14 – when he rode only one winner at Exeter, even though Pipe landed a treble.

So the stage was set for the Aintree confrontation the following week.

In the lead-up to Liverpool came the awards ceremony organised by the Jockeys' Association in the Hilton Hotel in London. They were in their second year. Dunwoody was the first winner of the National Hunt award in 1992. And was favourite to score a repeat – wihch he did – in '93.

Dunwoody and another jockey, Roger Marley, had decided to celebrate Dunwoody's performance and had ended up in the Plaza on Hyde Park Hotel in London's Bayswater Road. Needless to say, spirits were high and the police were eventually called after reports of rowdy behaviour. Eventually Marley and Dunwoody were taken to Paddington Green police station where they were arrested under the Public Order Act and cautioned before being released several hours later.

It was an unfortunate incident but Dunwoody to his credit cleared the air when he immediately issued a statement which read: "I deeply regret the incident early on Monday morning and the adverse publicity it might have brought to the ceremony and to my profession. I was upset at Roger Marley's arrest and this unfortunately led to my own."

And so ended an incident which was a temporary aberration in the career of a man who has always steered clear of controversy.

Dunwoody returned to the track at Sandown Park the day that he issued the statement and promptly rode a treble from his only three mounts – Amari King, Musthaveaswig and Shamana. This put him 17 clear of Scu.

The leading jockey at the Liverpool track in recent years, Dunwoody had notched up 13 winners since that memorable meeting when he won the National on West Tip. His first Liverpool winner was Glen Rue for Terry Casey, as mentioned already, and since then he had been the man to follow.

However, as was the case at Cheltenham '93, it all went wrong again. On the Saturday, Dunwoody was centre-stage as the focus of attention of half the sporting world as the Grand National descended into farce.

But even before the National itself Dunwoody knew it just wasn't going to be his meeting. Out of luck with no winners on the opening day – unusual for him – the rub of the green deserted him again on the second day which was spiked with tragedy and also came close to preventing Dunwoody turning out for the National at all.

He had high hopes that Waterloo Boy would recover his old form in the Mumm Melling Chase but just when he was going well in the lead the gelding burst a blood vessel and that put paid to a race Dunwoody might have won.

Worse, however, was to follow for in the Bell Epoque Sefton Novices Hurdle he was going well again on Now Your Talkin' for Nicky Henderson when the gelding dramatically collapsed in front of the stands with a broken leg and the dreaded green screens had to be brought out.

Dunwoody, who had been thrown to the ground, aggravated the broken bone in his hand and he had to pass a medical examination before he was allowed to take part in the National.

What National?

Yes, April 3, 1993 was the date of "the race which never was".

A day that will take a long time to live down by racing's Establishment and one which was watched in total bewilderment by millions.

The race was delayed first by protesters, then by two false starts and finally run off despite the efforts of officials around the track to stop the jockeys and inform them that their efforts were in vain. Eventually, John White, "the winning jockey" on Jenny Pitman's Esha Ness, a 50/1 chance, had to be told that all his efforts were for nought and that the race was void. You can picture his reaction, can't you?

But let's go back to the beginning of the whole sorry tale, to the time when 39 runners paraded in front of the stands and then began milling around in the starting area.

Everything seemed normal when starter Keith Brown called them into line. Chatam and Royle Speedmaster were giving some trouble. It looked as though the race would be off in time when Jamie Osborne and others began pointing down the course to warn the starter that protesters were in front of the first fence.

Eventually the animal rights protesters were removed and we were ready again. Nine minutes after the official "off" time the starter brought the horses into line but this time when he let them go, the tape, instead of catapulting out of the way, was caught up with several runners.

Brown kept his flag raised and shouted "False start" and 100 yards down the course Ken Evans, the recall man, raised his flag – according to some – and all the jockeys were able to return to the start. It had become a drama but the real crisis was waiting around the corner.

The tape was causing problems, having become weighed down because of the rain, and the fact that there was a high wind blowing didn't help matters either.

Four minutes later Brown called the riders into line again and let them go. But this time disaster struck – with Dunwoody right at the centre of it. The tape wrapped itself around Richard's neck and he was almost thrown to the ground as his mount,

Won't Be Gone Long, trod on another piece.

Again Brown shouted "False start" and raised his flag, only this time it appeared to be furled. Nine horses stayed where they were and the rest set off like the Charge of the Light Brigade with no apparent recall flag on display to tell them to pull up.

So off they went with the fascinated eyes of millions of television viewers watching every stride and not believing what they were seeing.

Bechers came and went, then Valentines and still no one pulled up. By this time officials were scurrying about everywhere and the huge crowd were catcalling. It was quite simply the most embarrassing nine minutes in British sport.

Coming to the Chair in front of the stands, some officials dashed out and tried to stop the "race" but it was no good. The riders continued oblivious of what was in front of them, jumped the Chair and went out into the country for the second time. No one could believe it. The whole place was a volcano of unreality.

Eventually, the "finish" involved Esha Ness, Cahervillahow, Romany King and The Committee who came home in that order, but by then the crowd were treating the whole affair like a huge joke. Boohs and catcalls for the starter and any other bowler-hatted official were the order of the day as the jockeys tried to explain why they didn't stop.

For many it was a case of believing that those trying to stop the race were protesters, and according to Charlie Swan, who rode Cahervillahow: "Going to the Chair I thought the animal rights people were still trying to stop us so I jumped to the left. The wind was whistling in my ears and it was very difficult to know what was going on."

Scu was one of those who pulled up after a circuit on Captain Dibble after he had been shouted at by Martin Pipe who gesticulated that the race was a non-starter.

Jenny Pitman, who trained the "winner", was beside herself with rage and charged into the weighroom during the farce demanding that the race be stopped – although that was what everyone apparently was trying to do. Afterwards there were scuffles and fights around the unsaddling enclosure before calmness was eventually restored.

Probably the best one-liner of the whole affair came afterwards from John White who, when asked why he didn't pull up when he realised he was virtually on his own, replied: "Have you ever ridden in the Grand National?"

And what of Dunwoody who was in a more subdued mood than most after having nearly been hanged? Richard pointed out in his calm and precise manner that he thought he heard a false start called the second time and told those jockeys nearest to him. However, he himself couldn't move because of the tape wrapped around him.

Later, after millions of words had been written in a matter of days, Dunwoody remarked to me: "You know there's no such thing as bad publicity. Look at the words that have been spewed out over the National. Personally, I think it will recover but the whole day was certainly a sad one for racing's image. Still, if it brings about a better method of starting then it will have done some good.

"Many have asked me what I would have done had I not been trapped by the tape and I can only say on reflection that I probably would have raced along with the rest and then pulled up after a circuit. You know, it's hard to stop once the adrenalin is thumping!"

CHAPTER 14

A WEEK TO MAKE UP
HIS MIND

Y ou couldn't describe it as an ultimatum as such. But the message was clear to Richard Dunwoody and every follower of National Hunt Racing.

'The Duke' Nicholson revealed that his No. 1 stable jockey had a week to make up his mind where he was hanging his boots the follow season.

There was no rift between the two. No breach in public. Absolutely no question of recriminations or sour grapes.

Nicholson, in effect, was laying his position clearly on the line in a totally factual manner. He wanted to know where he stood amid all the speculation surrounding the question: Would Dunwoody become the successor to Scudamore as No. 1 at the Pipe stable or would he maintain the status quo, utilising his talents principally for the Nicholson and Henderson stables?

Nicholson threw down the gauntlet, so to speak, two days after Dunwoody had been awarded the Whitbread Gold Cup on Topsham Bay following a Stewards inquiry.

The whole "will he, won't he?" saga rolled on to the Punchestown Festival meeting and on the first day – the Tuesday – Dunwoody rode his first Irish treble,including a victory for 'The Duke' on Viking Flagship in the BMW Drogheda Handicap Chase (he would complete a notable double on the same horse when taking the Bank of Ireland Colliers Novice Chase on the Thursday).

Interviewed after Dunwoody's success on Viking Flagship on the Tuesday, Nicholson said quite frankly: "The ball is in Richard's court. He must decide what he has to do."

And he added quizzically but quite significantly: "At the moment he is riding a lot of winners for me – so what could be wrong with that?"

And Henderson had reason to be pleased, too, for Dunwoody gave him his first Irish winner that memorable afternoon when Thinking Twice won the handicap hurdle.

Ultimately, everything would rest, of course,with Martin Pipe. Whoever got the call from him was going to find it very hard to refuse.

But he was playing his cards very close to his chest. Entering the Press room at Punchestown,he glanced at the stocky frame of Clement Freud and asked him with a mischievous gleam in his eye if he could do 10st 7lbs. To which Freud replied that he could barely do 17 stone!

Pipe wasn't revealing at that point whether or not he had made a concrete offer to Dunwoody – but within a fortnight – Tuesday, May 4th to be exact – it became known, without any official announcement, that the Pipe-Dunwoody link-up was a reality and soon Adrian Maguire had signed as the new No. 1 to the Nicholson stable.

Dunwoody when asked how he felt about the whole affair was once again the essence of diplomacy and steered clear of anything that might have got him into deep waters.

"I'm very much looking forward to the fresh challenge," he said. Mr. Pipe has made it clear that I may continue as many of my outside contacts as possible and together with their help it would be nice to crack the 200 one day."

At this stage Richard had ridden 155 winners and the big bookmakers were quick to state that in their view Dunwoody would be long odds on to retain the title in the 1993-'94 season.

There had been a few diehard supporters of Adrian Maguire prepared to take a price on the fact that Pipe might send for him – even if it was based more on hope than on conviction. They were reflecting no doubt on the time a famous phone call was made by Pipe to Homer Scott asking for a claimer to ride Omerta in the Kim Muir and Scott told him that Maguire was the best in Ireland and England.

Indeed, after Maguire had gone on after Cheltenham to win the Irish Grand National on Omerta for Pipe, Scott had exclaimed to me: "That's the best jockey to come out of Ireland since Jonjo O'Neill!"

But Pipe having weighed up all the factors, came down in favour of Dunwoody – and that was that.

I have little doubt in my mind that it was Dunwoody's burning ambition to remain as champion that swayed him to accept the Pipe offer. He indicated as much when he told me: "I want to be champion jockey and I'm willing to travel. You couldn't really call Mr. Pipe's stable run-of-the-mill in the sense that he just wins races with middle of the road horses. He has a lot of classy animals as well and I'm looking forward to riding them."

Then what about Waterloo Boy, Remittance Man or Carobee? "I'm disappointed at not being in a position to ride them, of course, but you can't have it every way," he added.

"I don't see any problem in commuting from my home to Mr. Pipe's stable and I feel we have a lot to offer each other."

And what of 'The Duke' Nicholson's reaction?

"Richard won the Jockeys' title from this stable and had a share in more prize money over the last three years than Peter Scudamore. I must admit that in view of that I didn't expect to see him go."

In fairness, however, Nicholson did point out that Pipe didn't come along and snatch Dunwoody. Nicholson and the jockey, he claimed, had been deep in negotiations – even before Scudamore announced his retirement.

"I wanted first claim on Richard for the 1993-'94 season," Nicholson explained. "I gave Richard time to think about it. This was before Scu retired. I approached Richard and he agreed to give it some thought. However, the weeks stretched and there was no decision so I felt I must know one way or the other pretty quickly. There was no mention of Pipe at that stage but later, of course, Richard, to his credit, kept me informed once Martin did come on the scene.

"I wish him well. We had seven great seasons together. He rode some fine races for me and I haven't changed my opinion that not only is he a great jockey, he's a gentleman as well."

Pipe naturally couldn't contain his glee. "It's great to have Richard working with us," he said. "He will be bringing some new ideas and new thoughts and I'm sure he will adapt to our methods. You know there were times during our discussions when I thought we would never get him. In the end we are very lucky."

Chester Barnes, former table tennis star and Pipe's assistant, summed it up when he said: "You couldn't buy him if he were a footballer for he would be valued at over £5m. In my view he is leaving the second best yard in the country for the best one in order to better himself. Could you blame him?"

Dunwoody could have been forgiven if he had taken things just that little bit more easily after signing up with Pipe. After all, he only had to run out the remainder of the season. He was already a mile in front in the race for the title.

Winner-seeking, however, has always spurred him on relentlessly, and he achieved his best ever May figure. Twenty-two winners were added to his score mainly through the injection of extra mounts from the Pipe stable.

"Martin's horses helped me keep up the momentum," he told me, "but I was also grateful for the support I received from my two retainers with David Nicholson and Nicky Henderson."

When the season came to its close early in June, Dunwoody was on a total of 173 winners. Ironically, he had ridden both at Stratford (afternoon) and Market Rasen (evening) on the last day for the season but was beaten on four favourites including Beech Road who looked certain to win at Stratford but was edged out on the line.

"I'm sorry I didn't win on one of those horses," he told me. "It would have been nice to have a winner on the final day but you can't have everything."

So one of the most dramatic seasons in the Dunwoody career ended with the Ulsterman champion jockey for the first time and, equally important from his point of view, linked to the champion trainer.

It seemed by the summer of 1993 that they had it made.

Looking back on that watershed 1992-'93 season, Dunwoody picked out one particular highlight which gave him great personal satisfaction and that was his first-day treble at Punchestown achieved through Bayrouge, Viking Flagship and Thinking Twice at the height of the speculation as to whether or not he would stay with Nicholson or move on. "I feel I rode that day better than at any time that season," he said. "I was really stoked up and it was important to win before the Irish public."

The smart money suggested at this time that if he steered clear of injury, it was highly unlikely that Dunwoody would be deprived of his crown in the immediate future. Indeed, he could look forward to adding appreciably to his tally of titles before he stepped down.

But he realised at the same time that, as in the case of the outstanding Nicholson horses he had said goodbye to riding, the greater demands that being No. 1 to the Pipe stable would impose could also lose him the ride on horses his name had become closely linked with in Ireland. It would all depend on when he was free and if he could continue to get over to Ireland for the big Sunday fixtures.

Dunwoody, for example, had built up a very happy partnership over fences with Flashing Steel, owned by former Irish Prime Minister, Charles J. Haughey and trained by his son-in-law, John Mulhern.

Mulhern does not suffer fools gladly in the racing business. The very fact that he decided that Dunwoody was the man to get the best out of Flashing Steel represents, I feel, one of the finest tributes of all to Richard's talent as a rider.

Flashing Steel began his career by winning three bumpers off the reel, at Leopardstown, Fairyhouse and Leopardstown again, before going hurdling at the beginning of 1992.

It was again the same story – three more wins off the reel with Kevin O'Brien his regular pilot before Flashing Steel met his first defeat when finishing 10th behind Thetford Forest – ridden by Dunwoody – in the Sun Alliance Novices Hurdle at Cheltenham. A mistake at the fourth just about put paid to his chances and in many ways this performance made Mulhern cautious about going to Cheltenham again until the gelding was fully grounded in the hurly-burly of the jumping game.

A third place behind Arthur Moore's Dee Ell at Fairyhouse in April of that year gave the impression that hurdling wasn't going to be Flashing Steel's forte anyway and the following November he was set to make his debut over fences.

The jockey for the occasion? Once again the call went out for Dunwoody.

"I reckoned I had the best young horse in Ireland and I wanted the best jockey," Mulhern told me. "so I rang up Richard and asked him to meet me. We had a chat at Bellewstown races and he said he would try to fit in the rides on Flashing Steel. He appeared to me to be a highly accommodating jockey who would do his best to help me if at all possible.

"To my mind he is simply the top jockey around. I felt the same when Tommy Carmody was in business and now that he has retired, Richard is the obvious choice as far as I am concerned. Hopefully he will continue to ride Flashing Steel for me even though he has a retainer with Pipe. With many major Irish races taking place on Sundays, Richard should be free."

Dunwoody rode Flashing Steel for the first time at Fairyhouse in November, 1992 and the partnership romped home by 20 lengths. After that they were on their way. Despite a fall at Punchestown the following month, Flashing Steel still looked the most exciting novice chaser in Ireland and he proved his ability twice more with Dunwoody up when winning the final of the Win Electric Chase series at Leopardstown in February and then the EBF Novice Chase Final at Fairyhouse later that month.

The pressure was on Mulhern to run at Cheltenham but he resisted it because as he put it: "Cheltenham has seen the ruination of many young horses. I am going to take my time with Flashing Steel and see what he's made of over fences. There are plenty of other races for him to run in at home."

Well, not everyone might have agreed with Mulhern's diagnosis of the Sun Alliance Novice Chase at Cheltenham but they had to respect his forthright views and his determination to do as he thought fit for the horse. Mulhern, therefore, decided to wait for Punchestown but as it turned out Dunwoody wasn't available, although he rode at the meeting.

The problem from Mulhern's point of view was that David Nicholson had decided to run Strong Beau, winner of the Kim Muir at Cheltenham in the Heineken Gold Cup Chase on the second day of the Festival and his was the race earmarked for Flashing Steel.

I spoke to Mulhern about riding plans shortly before the meeting and he assured me that Dunwoody would be riding for him. But when I spoke to Nicholson he told me that Dunwoody would be riding Strong Beau!

As for Richard, his reply was that he felt only one of the horses would run anyway and there was no point in getting involved in a two-way stretch early on.

Ultimately, both horses were declared with Dunwoody on Strong Beau and no jockey on Flashing Steel. Would Mulhern's horse run? Would there be a change of jockey at the last moment?

Mulhern was tight-lipped but eventually Tony Martin, arguably Ireland's top amateur rider, had the mount on Flashing Steel, for it was by now obvious that Nicholson was sticking to his retainer and Dunwoody had no option but to ride the stable horse.

At the end of the day neither horse won. Fissure Seal scored by a head from Son of War and in doing so provided a bitter sweet result for Charlie Swan who had ridden Fissure Seal to victory at Cheltenham. However, he had promised Dessie Hughes, the trainer of Dysart Lass, that he would ride his mare and Charlie wasn't going to go back on his word.

Dysart Lass finished fifth with Strong Beau sixth

and Flashing Steel a poor 12th after having received "reminders" early on.

A disappointing way to end what had been a fine season overall for the Mulhern horse.

But if there is one man who has no illusions about the racing game it is John Mulhern. He has forgotten more about it from his students days than many will ever learn . . . and the stories he can tell would fill a book in themselves . . . but then the best of them might not make his memoirs!

You can take it that Mulhern will always come bouncing back. And as he left Punchestown on that Wednesday evening, April 28th, 1993, he was naturally hoping that Flashing Steel, still only an eight-year-old would be back to win more races in the 1993-'94 season . . . and that Richard Dunwoody would be able to renew his partnership with the Broadsword gelding to win a few big ones.

CHAPTER 15

"THE MOST COMPLETE N.H. JOCKEY I HAVE SEEN"

Former Irish champion amateur jockey, Ted Walsh, who today combines the role of trainer with directing his talents towards television and journalism, reckons that Richard Dunwoody is the most complete National Hunt jockey he has ever seen.

"I sum up jockeyship in three categories – brains, horsemanship and riding strength. I think Richard has all three to the highest degree and he is the only jockey in my time of whom I could say that with such confidence," he said.

"You know there are many jockeys who have one and maybe even two of those components, but how many have the complete set? Dunwoody, in my view, is simply the best."

Naturally there can be no appraisal nowadays of the qualities of Richard Dunwoody as a jockey without making comparisons between him and Adrian Maguire.

Walsh is as forthright on this question as he is on all others. In Walsh's opinion, Maguire is unquestionably "a natural horseman" but he adds significantly: "He hasn't gone as far along the road as Richard has. Wait for another few years before you make up your mind about him. And you mustn't forget that Maguire is a natural jockey. He is built for the game because of his size. Dunwoody looks more like a rugby player, so you have to give him credit for what he has done.

"But most of all I pay tribute to his racing brain. I have seen the best of them from the latter days of Fred Winter down through the years when we had riders in Ireland like Frank Berry, Tommy Carberry and Tommy Carmody. None of them had a brain as sharp and as instinctive as Dunwoody.

"I recall him riding Second Schedual for Arthur Moore and it was well known that the gelding did not really stay three miles.

"The race was the Woodchester Rank Gold Cup at the 1992 Punchestown Festival meeting. Richard settled Second Schedual down nicely before bringing him on the scene approaching the last fence to go on and beat Charlie Swan on Open The Gate by a length. Jodami was third that day three and a half lengths behind – so it was quite a race.

"I've seen Richard work those tactics so often that I have to admire him for it. Yes, he has that in-built racing brain which only the best possess."

Richard Pitman, the former jockey and now a prominent racing interviewer with the BBC television team, believes that Adrian Maguire is "a talent going places" but Richard Dunwoody will remain champion for a few years before Adrian takes his measure.

"Maguire is quite simply a riding machine," he said. "He will go anywhere and ride any horse he is given. As he gets older, of course, this will change. But he has an advantage in that he is with David Nicholson who is one of many trainers taking on Pipe successfully. In addition, Maguire will

Richard Dunwoody wearing the overcoat of owner, Robert Waley-Cohen, to keep warm before the start of 'the National that never was' in 1993.

Below: Passing the winning line on West Tip when scoring his memorable Grand National triumph in 1986.

THE LONG ARM OF THE LAW . . . Colin Turner captures the moment when Richard Dunwoody is led away to meet the newspaper journalists after being interviewed by Des Lynam of the BBC (left).

Richard Dunwoody (left) as the victory champagne is produced and (right) receiving the winning jockey's trophy after West Tip's Grand National victory.

Richard Dunwoody on West Tip jumping the last in the 1989 National when he was runner-up and (inset), left, with the Ritz Club Trophy when top jockey at Aintree '91 and (inset) right, in familiar pose when doing a television interview.

West Tip (Richard Dunwoody), centre, proves what a great Aintree specialist he was as he clears the water in style on his way to finishing second to Little Polveir (Jimmy Frost), on inside, in the 1989 Grand National.

Richard Dunwoody's calling card to his former teachers in County Down, Kay McIlveen and May Lyttle after he had won the Grand National in 1986.

HAPPY FAMILY GATHERING . . . Richard Dunwoody's father, George is third from right (glasses) and his mother, Gillian third from left beside Betty Hill. His sister Gail is on extreme right. Second from left is Humphrey Graham, a cousin of George.

George Dunwoody leading in Billy Patton on Snow Finch after a point-to-point win in the early Sixties.

George Dunwoody (right), a very able rider in his day, leads the field in a point-to-point at Pigeonstown, County Antrim in the early Sixties.

HERE COMES THE BRIDE . . . Bernard Parkin records the joy of Richard Dunwoody and his bride, Carol on their wedding day in July, 1988.

Page, James Davies, son of jockey, Hywel, doesn't know quite what to make of the first (married) kiss and (right) West Tip turns up to offer his own special greeting.

Richard's mother Gillian, sharing her son's happiness on his wedding day as he welcomes another "surprise" guest, Charter Party.

HAIL THE CHAMPION . . . Richard Dunwoody has reason to smile as he holds the British N.H. Jockeys' Championship trophy and (right) fellow-Irishman Adrian Maguire, his great rival for the crown, giving a victory salute after winning the Gold Cup on Cool Ground in 1992.

FAREWELL TO SCU . . . Peter Scudamore pictured by Bernard Parkin on the day he retired from the saddle – April 7, 1993 – with Richard Dunwoody, the man who assumed his mantle.

also get many other spare rides. No, it's not a soft touch for Dunwoody at the top. Take it from me."

The self-critical element of Richard Dunwoody was brought very much to the fore by Pitman when he said: "You know, Richard comes home every night after racing and immediately settles down to watch videos of that day's contests so that he can analyse what he did wrong and hopefully try to improve his style.

"He will watch races where he feels he should not have won by so far and others where he might have won had he done something differently. I think that's important in a jockey, for when you cease to analyse your ability and try to correct your mistakes then that's the time you have stopped caring and you are only riding for the hell of it."

Pitman also feels that Dunwoody will not be champion as long as Francome and Scudamore.

"They were head and shoulders above their contemporaries but the competition, I feel, wasn't as hot in their day," he said. "Now Dunwoody has Maguire breathing down his neck and he has become champion just entering his thirties, which means that as time goes by the falls become harder.

"I'm not saying Richard is an old man. Far from it, for he has a lot of race riding to do before he eventually calls it a day. But if he had become champion in his early twenties then he could have looked more confidently at a long reign at the top.

"You know, Scu was lucky in that he came up with Martin Pipe. There was a great movement in the racing game in those days with pipe on the crest of a wave and Scu along with him. Although there's no doubt that Martin Pipe will still get his winners, I wonder is there the same hunger for victory or will the success tally flatten out. You can't expect to break records forever.

"Dunwoody also differs from Scu in that Peter was a whirlwind rider who thought everything out beforehand. Of course, Richard thinks as well, but you always knew when Peter was about to make his effort for he came on the scene like a tornado. In Dunwoody's case he is inclined to creep into a race and then suddenly he is in front. He prefers the rail on most occasions and there is no better rider on the inside."

Pitman feels that Dunwoody is reminiscent of Francome in one major respect. His presentation of a horse at a fence. "He does this brilliantly," he said. "Just watch him as he asks his mount for that last stride before take-off. Like Francome he is right down on the horse's withers and with a tight squeeze he is over. How often have you seen other jockeys sitting back or upright at a fence. Not Dunwoody or Francome."

Pitman has many vivid memories of Dunwoody at his best but one which always surges into his mind is that finish between Waterloo Boy and Barnbrook Again at Cheltenham. "You know there were some who had the view that Dunwoody's wasn't a great man in a finish but they changed their minds that day," Pitman said.

"Dunwoody was meeting probably the strongest finisher we have in Hwyel Davies but it didn't matter and he was only beaten in the final strides. Both jockeys got stood down after that race but that to my mind was a milestone in Dunwoody's career. It showed that as well as being stylish he also had guts when it mattered. Now he must be the best all-round jump jockey in Britain. Only time will tell if this is enough to keep him at the top."

One last observation from Pitman on another aspect of Dunwoody and Maguire – their ease with the interviewer and the obtrusive mike in the mouth and TV camera close up.

"Richard, as you know, is extremely articulate," Pitman said, "but Maguire was a nightmare in the early days. He just had nothing to say and appeared to be extremely shy, which no doubt he was. However, since he began to find his feet in England and get a lot of winners,he has begun to blossom and now we no longer dread having to go near him after a big race! From being a man who could barely put two words together Adrian has developed – or perhaps he has allowed to be uncovered – a sense of humour. His one liners can be quite funny and happily he does not take himself too seriously. That would be disastrous."

David Elsworth, the man who brought about;the partnership of Dunwoody and the nation's favourite Desert Orchid, has no doubts about what makes Dunwoody great. "Durability and concentration," he told me. "Those two factors are the secret of his success and they also contributed to Scu winning so many races and staying champion for so long.

"Dunwoody and Scudamore would have ridden more horses in a week than I would have ridden in half a season," he joked. "Anyone else would have got tired of going to the same tracks and meeting the same fences day in and day out. As in most other sports the concentration would have snapped at some stage but this never seemed to happen. The pair of hem appeared to enjoy race riding and quite honestly, I don't know how they maintained their sanity. You take it. Six days a week for something like 10 months of the year. It's enough to drive you round the bend!

"I remember years ago I was a great fan of Martin Molony who was a house guest with me not so long ago. Back in the Fifties, Martin, who was champion jockey in Ireland and second in England, used to travel over on the ferry to race here and he never seemed to get tired of this arduous grind.

"But the number of horses he rode wouldn't begin to compare with the total facing Scu and Dunwoody. Two hundred winners is now a reasonable target. This was unheard of in the days of Fred Winter and Molony, although Martin set up many records in Ireland, so I suppose you have to take his Irish total along with the one in England.

"But the pace of life is faster these days. You can't dispute this and I think that Dunwoody deserves the highest credit for the way in which he has dedicated himself to be champion. He shows no signs of letting up but I for one was surprised when he took the Pipe job for I felt it meant he was abandoning many of the quality horses he had been associated with.

"This move on his part showed how much he wanted to remain champion. He didn't mind the grind. He just wanted winners. It's that outlook which will make him very hard to beat."

Elsworth thinks it was a wise move on Maguire's part to join the Nicholson stable as No. 1 jockey.

"David Nicholson will iron out any of the rough edges which are still with him. He has an awe-inspiring natural talent and I feel he will become more of the complete jockey once he forgets about waving that whip."

Elsworth went on to make the interesting point that Richard Dunwoody might not continue to have the same incentive to remain champion, for once you have achieved something there is a feeling of anti-climax. What else is there after all except staying in the one place? Once you've become champion you've got nothing left to achieve. This is where Dunwoody is going to have his problems. Maintaining the momentum.

"Still he has proved to be a marvellous big race jockey and I am as intrigued as anyone else to see how many winners he can produce through the 'Pipe line'. Richard obviously feels he has made the right move and he knows his own business best. But the path to further championships may not be as smooth as many were predicting at the beginning of the 1993-'94 season."

Toby Balding was on the spot when Adrian Maguire hit the headlines as the new "wonder boy" of the National Hunt scene and he helped lift the young Irishman with the boundless energy and enthusiasm to greater heights as the trainer of Cool Ground which Adrian rode to a brilliant triumph over French-trained The Fellow in the 1992 Gold Cup.

"I would describe Dunwoody as a jump jockey who rides with a Flat racing style," he told me. "He's the best in that category since Johnny Haine and Graham Bradley Just watch the way he races. He sits further down into a horse than most jockeys in the National Hunt game. You would know him anywhere.

"In addition, he doesn't bully his horses.On the contrary, he has great sympathy with them. Horses always have something left in the tank after a Dunwoody ride for he usually has them where he wants them during a race.

"Many times I have watched him sum up the opposition in a flash and very quickly seize an opportunity to move into the right position at the right time. This is his great strong point.

"In addition he now has a few miles on the clock. he is no longer the youngster he was a few years ago. I would say now he is the complete performer, matching talent with total experience. No trainer could wish for more.

"I'll always remember him riding Beech Road for me in the SW Showers Silver Trophy at the Cheltenham April meeting in 1993. He had never sat on the horse before and I had told Richard that we always held him up and kept him off the pace. But after Beech Road had 'banked' the second fence, Richard grabbed the opportunity to send him on and he made all the running from that stage to win. It was quite simply a superb ride on a horse who had suffered a lot of problems.

"You know, Dunwoody appears to click with a horse first time, which is an unusual knack. Take Morley Street for example. I reckoned the former Champion Hurdler was made for him, for he had to be turned off and then on again and this was something Richard could do to perfection. In those races on Morley Street he showed what I would call the Bradley style, although I have to add that I felt he came too soon on Morley Street that day at Liverpool when Minorette's girl nearly caught him.

"To me, Dunwoody rides a stylish finish on all occasions and that's why I compare him to Bradley rather than John Francome. I always felt that John lacked Flat racing dash at the finish of his races, but of course he usually had them won out in the country where there was simply no one any better.

"As for Maguire, I feel it is fair to say that his one great motivation is enthusiasm. I have never seen anyone who gets such a buzz out of race riding as he does. Whereas Richard will comeback with that unruffled look, Adrian always appears to be bursting with the sheer thrill of competition. He will ride anywhere. He simply loves the game and I can see him giving Richard some problems in the years ahead.

"Their styles are also markedly different, for Adrian's is more upright, before he flattens out when he gets into the drive position as they call it. Perhaps it's because any falls he has had have resulted in him injuring his back, but he does have a style of riding you could identify a long way off.

"Both jockeys have that indefinable flair which is essential in any sport, but whereas Richard came from a racing background and had his talent nurtured and developed along the way, Adrian appeared on the scene like a meteor. I reckon we are lucky to be able to watch two such great riders in action these days. Personally I would be pleased to have either of them riding my Gold Cup hope."

CHAPTER 16

"WINTER BETTER THAN DUNWOODY – AND ALL THE REST"

Lord Oaksey had no hesitation in responding to the question when I asked him if Richard Dunwoody was the best National Hunt jockey ever? "No way. That honour belongs to Fred Winter."

Oaksey did, however, concede that Dunwoody is "the most complete jockey in the National Hunt game today."

Developing his argument as to why Fred Winter has to be given the accolade as the best ever, he said: "Dunwoody is as fine an all round horseman as you'll see," he told me. "He's stylish and is very rarely in the wrong position in a race. But when it comes to the best man in a finish I can't forget Fred. He was really something else.

"I remember some years ago when John Francome was champion jockey I talked to Fred about John's ability and I told him 'If you and John were on similar horses both reacting the same way to the going and you arrived neck and neck three fences or hurdles from home, I would have the mortgage on you to win.'

"Fred didn't see it that way for he said: 'Yes, but

don't forget you have to work out how much ground John would have gained on his horse out in the country so that he would be that much fresher than mine by the time it came to the closing stages.'

"If memory serves me correctly I can't recall Dunwoody riding a bad race. I feel he will be a first rate champion in the tradition of Winter and Stan Mellor."

Which brought us back to the immortal Fred again and one other piece of reminiscing from the noble Lord. "Who can forget that 1961 Gold Cup when Fred rode Saffron Tartan against Dave Dick on Pas Seul," he said. "Saffron Tartan was legless at the last but Fred still won. Afterwards Dick said 'you don't have to ask who's best now, do you'!"

Controversy over the use or misuse of the whip didn't make headlines in the era when Lord Oaksey – then Mr. John Lawrence – was riding Carrickbeg in the 1963 Aintree Grand National and was narrowly beaten in a desperately-close finish by 66/1 outsider Ayala. But the Channel 4 racing personality and prominent journalist holds very strong views on this subject – and is fearless in expressing them.

"Legs and body were what /Winter and later Jeff King used in their strongest finishes," he told me. "Nowadays many jockeys seem to regard the whip as the only method to get a horse home.

"However, I must state here and now that Dunwoody's whip style is misleading and that's why he has run foul of the stewards on some occasions. He gives the impression sometimes that he is hitting a horse when in fact he is only waving the whip. The stewards have misinterpreted his methods."

Lord Oaksey reckons that if Dunwoody hits it off with Pipe then there is nothing to stop him being champion jockey for a long time to come.

"I know Maguire has youth on his side and with his enthusiasm which is infectious to a horse," he said. "In fact, every ride he takes he regards as a winner. But that won't always be the case. In addition, he has over used the whip in my view and I am glad to see that he is learning to control this tendency. With David Nicholson on his side I see him getting a lot of winners in the years ahead but Dunwoody must be favourite to stay in front while Pipe is around.

Eddie Harty knows all about Fred Winter for he has been a close friend of Fred's for many years and sold him a lot of good horses. Like Lord Oaksey, Eddie regards Fred as the best but he makes an intriguing point about riding styles these days, particularly where they concern Dunwoody.

"Jockeyship has changed from my day," said the Kildare trainer who won the National for Toby Balding on Highland Wedding in 1969. "Richard rides with a long rein with a distinct 'loop' in it. It's a quiet style, giving him a loose hold of the horse's head. I my day it was different. We were told to keep a firm grip of the horse's head at all times.

"Still, Dunwoody appears perfectly relaxed and in control with that loose rein approach and he certainly gets results form his horses.

"Fred Winter was more my type of jockey. He loved to get the inside and was always in the first four or five. Horses conserved their energies for him and when he was in a tight finish he was the man to beat. I thought he had no peers when he was in touch jumping the last fence."

"Martin Molony was another fiercely competitive rider and more in the Adrian Maguire style than the Dunwoody mould. He too rode with a loose rein, would you believe, but you never noticed any 'loop'. Martin had beautiful hands and had horses lobbing along and seemingly doing nothing. Then he galvanised them in a finish and apart from Winter I can think of no one who was so difficult to beat. He had complete dedication and will to win.

"You know, Martin was apprenticed to my father and I used to ride out with him and Paddy Moylan. My first race at Naas saw me lining up with Martin on one side and Jimmy Brogan on the other. I was 14 at the time and my father told me I would get through the race in one piece because of my two "minders". Well he was right, for although I didn't win I finished the course.

"That was 40 years ago but I still have vivid memories of that day."

Eddie was the first man I spoke to in connection with the great jump jockeys who mentioned the word "genius" when referring to Dunwoody. But he applied it to Molony and Winter as well.

"Fred and Martin had that certain something which made horses run more quickly than they would normally and Dunwoody has it as well," he said. "I suppose you could put it down to great hands. Without this talent you can't get horses to settle and you can't get them to pick up when you want them to. Dunwoody looks the perfect rider in this respect and I have always felt that his rides on Desert Orchid were beautiful to watch for there was a flow in the movement which was almost artistic.

"Molony and Winter were more the aggressive type of race rider and as I've said Maguire appears to be set to follow them. He has an irresistible will to win, but then he's the sort of rider who shows his emotions. Richard on the other hand is a cool customer but that doesn't mean that his heart is not beating on overtime as well."

Eddie also mentioned the fact that jockeys – including Dunwoody – ride much shorter nowadays than when Winter and Molony were in their prime, but that's the way the sport changes. And that's what gives it variety.

"At the end of the day, I'd probably plump for Fred as having the edge on the rest," he added, "but there was little in it between him, Terry Biddlecombe, John Francome and Tim and Martin Molony and you certainly cannot make accurate comparisons between riders of a previous generation and today's crop. It's like comparing boxers. It's just impossible. But it's fascinating to talk about!"

John Francome was seven times champion jockey until he just got fed up with the grind and gave it all up in the mid-Eighties. Now he is in the position to look at other jockeys and as a television commentator he has won a special niche in the racing game.

His pointed and witty comments are highly valued for everyone knows that John can spot a phoney a mile off and he's not afraid to say so. As he told me: "Dunwoody is like all the top jump jockeys. He has no airs and graces and just gets on with the job. Try talking to some of the top Flat jockeys and see how far you get. Some of them wouldn't give you the time of day!"

Francome is the yardstick by whom all the leading jockeys of recent years are judged but he is modest enough to suggest that Dunwoody might just be a better pilot than he was. "He's a superb stylist," John told me. "The complete jockey and I am delighted that he made it to the top. I see him being champion for many years yet even though the Martin Pipe stable is bound to level out for nothing goes on forever.

"Dunwoody is marvellous at presenting a horse to a fence and he has retained that eagerness which you must have to be champion jockey. He would ride in six or seven races seven days a week and go anywhere in order to grab those mounts. That's what you must do if you are to be champion. That's the way I was when I was top of the table. I thought nothing of long distance travel. Then one day I tired of doing the same thing every day and decided to give it all up. I have no regrets."

Francome is convinced that Adrian Maguire is a clone of Jonjo O'Neill. "Everything about Maguire tells me that he is another Jonjo," he told me. "Like Fred Winter he regards every fence as only a minor and relatively unimportant obstacle on the way to the winning post. He rides as though the fences aren't there at all! It's truly amazing.

"Of course I see him being a threat to Dunwoody in the years to come, but Richard is also hungry for winners and he won't be dislodged as easily as some might like to make out."

I asked him the inevitable question about comparing riders but he refused to be drawn. "Every era throws up its champions," he said. "I never really paid much attention to Fred Winter when he

196

was in his heyday. I was probably too young! But those who were his contemporaries are convinced that he was the greatest.

"That may be so but in more recent years we have had jockeys like Jeff King and David Mould who were just as strong in a finish as Fred and had tremendous all round style. Dunwoody is fit to rank with these riders and also with my good friend Scu of course. But to compare him with Scu would do neither a favour. They are different types of jockeys with very little between them when it comes to pure talent. I wouldn't put one ahead of the other.

"You know, we are very fortunate these days in that we have riders like Dunwoody, Maguire and Mark Dwyer whom I reckon are the best three in Britain. They have made the jump game more exciting than it has been for many years."

Dermot Weld has been quoted as saying that he regarded Maguire as the best jump jockey in the world. Dermot,however, regards this statement as a certain amount of journalistic licence. "What I did say was that Adrian was ONE of the best in the world," he said. "In time he may yet turn out to be the greatest but that's still to be decided."

Meantime, Weld was unsparing in his admiration for Dunwoody whom he described as having an "enormous talent in the classic mould."

And he added the view that he felt Dunwoody was a better rider than either Francome or Scudamore. "Both Francome and Scudamore had talent like Dunwoody's but I firmly believe that Dunwoody is a more stylish exponent of the art of race riding and that being the case I would put him at the top of the list," he added.

"I think as long as he stays free from injury he has the ability to remain champion for a long time. His success is based on coolness under pressure, intelligence, patience and determination.

"You know, I rode against his father George and I am a close friend of the family. In fact, my late father and my mother had long lasting links with George and his wife Gillian.

"George is a nice man and was a fine rider but there was no similarity in styles, although like Richard he had a highly developed racing brain. He also, as I found out on one occasion, had a useful tongue and I was at the receiving end of it, although I stress that it was very much my own fault.

"I remember riding at Sligo and I cut across George on a bend. I had no sooner done so than this Northern voice let loose at me to show me exactly what George thought about my taking such liberties.

"George was fuming and for the life of me I can't remember whether or not my manoeuvre paid off!

"Still, he had every reason to be angry on that occasion although we always remained good friends and I am proud to say have remained so ever since.

"It was no surprise to me when Richard became the high class jockey he is today for his parents came from the best of racing stock.

"As for young Maguire, well what can you say about a man who doesn't appear to know what defeat is like? At his age his talent is exceptional with a wonderful eye for a jump. He is also totally fearless and has that priceless knack of getting horses round with the minimum of fuss.

"Pat Taaffe was like that. Many said Pat couldn't ride a finish but he had a tremendous knack of putting horses right at a fence and this was where he won his races.

"In time Maguire could take over from Dunwoody but not just yet for Richard is much more polished and Maguire still has a long way to go in this respect. Still, he is brushing up his technique all the time and before long he could be in the position Dunwoody is in now."

Former Irish champion jockey Tommy Carberry also remembers riding against Dunwoody's father George and reckons that father and son had a lot in common.

"What I recall is that George used his head during a race," he said. "He knew the horse he was riding, was well aware of its capabilities and knew where to place it during a race to get the best out of it. I didn't ride all that much against him for our careers only briefly overlapped, but I always thought he was a highly intelligent man and Richard is very much a similar type of jockey, the only difference being that while George was obviously more amateurish in style Richard has all the professional touches.

"Where Richard excels is out in the country where he gets the best out of a horse. I'll always remember his rides on Charter Party in the Gold Cup and, of course, West Tip in the National. He reminded me very much of Pat Taaffe in his prime as far as pure horsemanship is concerned. If you are riding in the National you have to make sure your horse has every chance of getting the trip for this is probably the most important aspect of the race these days. Dunwoody is superb at making up ground almost unnoticed and then arriving with a double handful at just the right time. He did this especially with West Tip in 1986 and when I saw him that day I knew he had a future."

Tommy reckons that Dunwoody will be champion for a long time even though Maguire is snapping at his heels.

"I put Maguire down as a Fred Winter type rider, all action and never giving up when given the slightest chance. Dunwoody is more a stylist in the fashion of Josh Gifford and Terry Biddlecombe.

"If I had to point to the National and Gold Cup as Dunwoody's two most memorable rides, then I must go for the Gold Cup and the Irish National in the case of Maguire.

"In both cases he showed great perseverance and simply refused to recognise that he might be beaten either on Cool Ground or Omerta. That's what makes Maguire such a tough opponent, and it will be intriguing to see both Dunwoody and Maguire in their head to head contests as the seasons unfold.

"Personally I would like to be riding against them these days. I only wish I were 20 years younger. You would have seen some action!"

CHAPTER 17

ALL OUR BIRTHDAYS
AND ALL THAT!

The autumn leaves had begun to fall and the 1993-'94 National Hunt season would soon be in full swing. Richard Dunwoody's 30th birthday was looming on January 18, 1994.

He had now entered that phase of his career when he was right at the peak of his profession and reigning champion. But deep down he had got to realise that time was no longer on his side as it was in the case of Adrian Maguire, for example.

As Richard Pitman has pointed out – and he should know from experience – the falls become harder to take when you enter your thirties. When Jayne Thompson was killed back in 1986 – the year Dunwoody won the Grand National on West Tip – John Karter wrote that "it must have made every rider stop and take a long pause for hard thought."

Dunwoody, without appearing in any way unfeeling, gave this reaction: "I didn't know Jayne and obviously it shocks you more when it's someone you know, like my friend Michael Blackmore, who was killed at Market Rasen a few years ago."

Then he added very significantly: "But you can't let yourself think about it. You have to put it out of your mind or you'd give up."

When you reflect on Niall Madden and Tommy Carmody being forced into premature retirement through injury and earlier of Tommy Carberry, one of the most brilliant of National Hunt riders, lying in hospital in Listowel, almost at death's door after a horrific fall – and then calling it a day – you realise that Dunwoody's career has been conspicuously free of the kind of falls that shatter a man's nerve.

For Dessie Hughes, who won the Gold Cup on Davy Lad in 1977 and the Champion Hurdle on Monksfield in 1979 after an epic battle with Jonjo O'Neill on Sea Pigeon from the last flight, has said that it's how a rider comes back from the bad falls that counts for everything in the end. Some are broken mentally. It becomes obvious to their peers that they can no longer go into fences as they used to and once the nerve is gone it's all up for them really.

Not that Dunwoody has not had his share of falls. John Karter noted that back in one week in 1986 he had a heavy fall five days out of six, one just half an hour before he climbed back into the saddle to ride one of the best races of that same season on Church Warden at Ascot. "In the world of the India rubber man, he appears to bounce better than most," added Karter. Resilience could well be his middle name.

No one has ever doubted Dunwoody's fearlessness or his courage and Peter Scudamore went on record to describe him as "a very brave rider."

Ironically, the famous gap-toothed grin that first became known to millions when he was interviewed on television after his Grand National triumph in 1986 seemed to indicate to the world that the tooth was lost in a fall in some chase, away from the frenetic excitement of Aintree.

But, no, it was lost in the school playground on the day he also suffered a broken nose.

Ambition was always a smouldering flame burning in Richard Dunwoody's soul. Indeed, Capt. Tim Forster said he discerned "a burning ambition" from the very first day that the Ulsterman joined his stable.

The key to Dunwoody and what has spurred him right through his career can be found in his statement in 1986: "I want to be champion jockey more than anything. It means more to me even than winning the National."

That was a clear statement of intent – a warning to all the other jockeys in the weighroom.

Behind the easy-going public persona he presented, you might even describe it as self-effacing, Dunwoody had immense belief and confidence in his own talent and ability. And this was cemented further after his triumph on West Tip and later his Gold Cup victory on Charter Party, leading on to the completion of the "Big Three" when Kribensis won the Champion Hurdle.

But he had not reckoned with Peter Scudamore forming a partnership with Martin Pipe that, in effect, made it impossible for any other jockey to compete on level terms, for the flow of winners coming from the "Pipe line" was such that no matter how much of a tally Dunwoody notched up, he would have to be content with second place.

John Karter wrote in the *Sunday Times* in December, 1990 that "with the greatest respect to Scudamore, undoubtedly one of the most gifted National Hunt riders of the modern era, his unprecedented numerical supremacy owes much to an unfair advantage. That is the only way to describe his association with Martin Pipe, the record-breaking Somerset trainer who has swept them both into jump racing history with a flood-tide of winners."

And Karter summed up: "Jenny Pitman once said that the only way to stop Pipe would be to send in the SAS. Dunwoody, who has never made any secret of his hunger for the jockeys' title, must have felt the same way about Scudamore."

Even when he still led Scudamore entering the climactic stage of the 1992-'93 season, the fear was there haunting Dunwoody through his waking hours that he would be caught at the death and once again denied the crown he had aspired to for so long.

Scudamore's sudden decision to retire saved him having to endure further frustration and disappointment in his quest for his first title.

The very fact that he was handed it, to all intents and purposes, rather than winning it in a tense battle all the way to the wire made some cynics liken it to a cardboard replica. But Dunwoody could counter that by claiming that if you took out the "Pipe line" factor he would have been champion much earlier and anyway he had certainly earned his first crown the hard way.

It was clear then that whoever had the "Pipe line" in his favour was going to farm the championship title – that is assuming Pipe continued to turnout the winners on a level commensurate with previous seasons, even without creating new records and injury was avoided by Pipe's No. 1.

Therefore, when Pipe made his offer to

Dunwoody to take over as No. 1 in succession to Scu, the ambition that had been part and parcel of Dunwoody's make-up from the moment he set his foot on the ladder compelled him to give a positive response.

In a word, Dunwoody had no intention of losing the crown by default to Adrian Maguire or any other jockey simply because he spurned the Pipe offer. If you went with Pipe, you would more than likely keep the title in the years ahead – as Scu had farmed it when No. 1 to the Somerset trainer – and if you said 'No' to the offer, your ambitions would have to lie elsewhere.

But in the final analysis the question came down to this: Had Dunwoody in his desire to remain champion taken the right road? Had he settled for the 'numbers game' rather than deciding coldly that his thirties would see him aiming as much as possible for the big targets on the best horses he could get to ride, even outside his own retainers?

Dunwoody argues that Pipe unquestionably has some of the best. The victory of Granville Again in the 1993 Champion Hurdle was indicative of the fact that the stable has the "ammunition" to enable him to land prizes that matter. Then there's the enigmatic Carvills Hill . . .

But there are those who would counter this argument by contending that once you team up with Pipe you get caught on a treadmill, on a merry-go-round that seems never-ending in its quest for winners that can come from out-of-the-way tracks in nameless races that bear no comparison to the adrenalin-pumping pitch of Cheltenham in March or Aintree for that matter.

And Dunwoody himself has confessed that

Cheltenham is "the Mecca" of the National Hunt game and the greatest meeting of all in the calendar year.

Dunwoody has proved himself a big-race jockey *par-excellence.* Lester Piggott, it will be recalled, broke with Noel Murless back in the Sixties in order to be free to pick and choose. And it led on to his riding the best Classic winners from the Vincent O'Brien stable, to Epsom Derby triumphs on Sir Ivor (1968), Nijinsky (1970), Roberto (1972) and The Minstrel (1977) that can never be forgotten, not to mention the Arc victories on Alleged (1977 and '78) and the Washington DC International Stakes on Sir Ivor in 1968.

One could venture that once Dunwoody has become champion once, it doesn't really matter what sequence of title wins he runs up. What is far more likely to be remembered is every brilliant ride he produces and every outstanding victory he scores, especially on top horses.

Pat Taaffe is remembered not for the number of winners he amassed in the course of his career (did it matter in his case, anyway?) but for his partnership with the peerless Arkle and that first great triumph over Mill House in the Cheltenham showdown that the Gold Cup became in 1964 ("Play the video again for me, Sam . . ."). Those who were there will never forget the 'Irish roar' that erupted as Arkle came down the hill. It was not equalled until Jonjo O'Neill gave his arm-aloft-victory-salute-to-the-heavens when passing the post on Dawn Run in the 1986 Gold Cup.

Yes, moments like that are more important than any championship title because they are the moments that make National Hunt racing what it is for so many.Richard Dunwoody made his choice after careful thought – and the decision was his and his alone.

Men will go on debating whether he made the right one.

Each birthday, after he has celebrated his 30th birthday on January 18, 1994 will bring him nearer the day of retirement.

Every birthday from this out will have its own significance.

Outside of the titles won, how will his reputation have been enhanced through the seasons of his thirties . . . and what never-to-be-forgotten moments will he leave us to remember and cherish?

You can only ponder. What remains is what he stitched into the record in 1986: "I want to be champion jockey more than anything else. It means more to me than winning the National."

He was bred to be a champion. And he is THE champion.

THE RICHARD DUNWOODY RECORD – *MAJOR RACES WON*

Mackeson Gold Cup at Cheltenham:
Very Promising..1986
Another Coral...1991

H. and T. Walker Handicap Chase at Ascot:
Church Warden 1986

Gerry Feilden Hurdle at Newbury:
Kribensis...1988
Mighty Mogul 1992

William HIll Handicap Hurdle at Sandown:
Prideaux Boy 1984

Tripleprint Handicap Chase at Cheltenham:
Another Coral...1992

King George VI Rank Chase at Kempton:
Desert Orchid 1989
Desert Orchid 1990

Top Rank Christmas Hurdle at Kempton:
Kribensis...1988

Kribensis...1989
Mighty Mogul 1992

Rowland Meyrick Handicap Chase at Wetherby:
The Thinker...1986

Black & White Whisky Champion Chase
at Leopardstown:
Very Promising...1986

Mildmay Cazalet Handicap Chase at Sandown:
West Tip..1985
Mr. Frisk 1989

Victor Chandler Handicap Chase at Ascot:
Waterloo Boy 1992

Arlington Premier Chase Final at Newbury:
Remittance Man 1992

Charterhouse Mercantile Chase at Cheltenham:
West Tip..1985

Agfa Diamond Chase at Sandown:
Charter Party 1988
Desert Orchid 1991

Agfa Hurdle at Sandown:
Celtic Chief 1988

Game Spirit Chase at Newbury:
Very Promising...1988
Waterloo Boy 1992
Waterloo Boy 1993

Tote Gold Trophy Handicap Hurdle at Newbury:
Grey Salute..1989

Racing Post Handicap Chase:
Desert Orchid 1990

Arkle Trophy Chase at Cheltenham:
Waterloo Boy 1989
Remittance Man 1991

Grand Annual Chase at Cheltenham:
French Union 1987

Sun Alliance Novices Hurdle at Cheltenham:
Thetford Forest...1992

**Coral Golden Handicap Hurdle Final at
Cheltenham:**
Von Trappe..1985

Triumph Hurdle at Cheltenham:
Kribensis...1988

**Ritz Club National Hunt Handicap Chase at
Cheltenham:**
West Tip..1985
Bigsun 1990

Champion Hurdle at Cheltenham:
Kribensis...1990

Cheltenham Gold Cup:
Charter Party 1988

County Handicap Hurdle at Cheltenham:
Thumbs Up 1993

Festival Bumper at Cheltenham:
Montelado..1992

Seagram Top Novices Hurdle at Liverpool:
Carobee..1992

Martell Cup Chase at Liverpool:
Aquilifer 1991

John Hughes Memorial Trophy Handicap Chase at Liverpool:
Glenrue..1986
Won't Be Gone Long...1990
The Antartex 1992

Mumm Melling Chase at Liverpool:
Remittance Man 1992

Martell Aintree Hurdle at Liverpool:
Celtic Chief 1988
Morley Street 1992

Martell Grand National at Liverpool:
West Tip...1986

Irish Grand National at Fairyhouse:
Desert Orchid 1990

BMW Champion Novice Hurdle at Punchestown:
High Plains 1987
The Proclamation..1989
Bayrouge 1993

Whitbread Gold Cup at Sandown:
Topsham Bay 1993

BMW Handicap Chase at Punchestown:
Viking Flagship 1993
Bank of Ireland Novice Chase at Punchestown:
Viking Flagship 1993

Breeders Cup Chase (U.S.A.):
Highland Bud..1989
Highland Bud..1992

Colonial Cup (U.S.A.):
Highland Bud..1989

Other Achievements:
Most wins in a British season...............173 (1992-'93)
Number of Centuries...4
Five wins in a day ....Chepstow, Nov. 7, 1992
Champion Jockey (races won).......................1992-'93
Champion Jockey (money won):
...........................1989-'90, 1990-'91, 1991-'92, 1992-'93

Career Totals:
1982-'83...4
1983-'84...24
1984-'85...46
1985-'86...55
1986-'87...70
1987-'88...79
1988-'89...91
1989-'90...102
1990 '91..127
1991-'92...137
1992-'93...173